THE LAST GREAT
DINOSAURS

A Guide to the Dinosaurs of Alberta

Monty Reid

Illustrations by
Jan Sovak

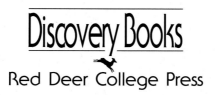

Discovery Books

Red Deer College Press

THE PUBLISHERS
Red Deer College Press
56 Avenue & 32 Street Box 5005
Red Deer Alberta Canada T4N 5H5

CREDITS
DESIGN   Blackbird Design
TYPESETTING   Boldface Technologies Inc.
PRINTED & BOUND
IN SINGAPORE FOR   Red Deer College Press

CANADIAN CATALOGUING IN PUBLICATION DATA
Reid, Monty, 1952-
The last great dinosaurs
ISBN 0-88995-055-5
1.Dinosaurs. I.Title.
QE862.D5R44 1990 567.9'1 C90-091419-X

10   9   8   7   6   5   4   3   2   1

Acknowledgements

Many people have been involved in this project. Without their generous assistance, *The Last Great Dinosaurs* could not have been written. Darren Tanke and Donna Sloan provided ideas and enthusiasm in the early going. The librarians at the Royal Tyrrell Museum of Palaeontology, in particular Joanne Lavkulich and Connie Hall, were unflappable and unfailing in their support. Many others, including Becky Kowalchuk, Linda Strong-Watson, Brooks Britt and Dr. Dennis Braman, gave information, good cheer and timely criticism.

Kevin Aulenbach was a bracing, generous and unflinchingly sober companion on many evenings when the project seemed moribund. Dr. David Eberth checked the dates and demonstrated how dinosaurs walked on their toes. Dr. Donald Brinkman wrenched himself away from a study of fossil turtles to provide new dinosaurian insights. Vital assistance came from Dr. Philip Currie, whose enthusiasm for dinosaurs is unmistakable and contagious. He commented on manuscript, maps and illustrations and was generous with dinosaur lore, thus providing invaluable support in spite of a demanding schedule.

Ken Uyeda, the designer of this book, gave much-appreciated advice throughout the evenings and weekends. A debt is also owed to the late artist Zdenek Burian, whose life and discipline provided the artist with enduring inspiration and guidance.

We take pleasure in acknowledging a debt to the Royal Tyrrell Museum of Palaeontology. The Tyrrell's dinosaurs got us hooked. Few museums are so exciting or so satisfying. Special thanks is also due to Dennis Johnson of Red Deer College Press, whose energy brought the entire project together in the end.

Last but not least, Patricia Wood and Daniela Sovak's patience and support were unstinting. Thanks.

– *Monty Reid & Jan Sovak*

The publishers gratefully acknowledge the financial contribution of the Canada Council, the Alberta Foundation for the Literary Arts, Alberta Culture and Multiculturalism, Red Deer College and Radio 7 CKRD

Special thanks to Vicki Mix, Pat Roy, Nicole Markotic and Carolyn Dearden for their assistance in preparing this book for publication.

Contents

Contents

We often wonder why dinosaurs are so popular. They capture the imagination of young and old around the world in a way that no other extinct animals ever have. Why should we care? They're dead, so what does it matter? But why, we continue to ask, why did they die? Few questions in science have been asked as often as this one. Perhaps this in itself in part explains the popularity of these almost mythical animals.

The Red Deer River has cut deep into the prairies of western Canada to expose the last chapters of dinosaurian history in a manner unparalleled anywhere else. Only the last fifteen million years, of a history that is ten times that long, of dinosaur time are documented along the two hundred kilometer stretch of river from the city of Red Deer to where the waters merge with those of the South Saskatchewan. But even within that relatively short distance, the changes are startling.

In the south, the badlands of Dinosaur Provincial Park show that dinosaurs had reached their peak seventy-five million years ago. More than thirty-five species lived in the area. They had reached a peak of sophistication previously unseen. All were better adapted for running and walking than their forebears. Some had brains comparable to those of the mammals and birds of the time. The rapidly growing babies of at least some species were protected and cared for by one or both of their parents. Fantastic crests, frills and horns developed on many, perhaps to help them identify each other as they moved in enormous herds across the landscape. And move they did. Alberta lay at the crossroads of dinosaurs travelling north to the Arctic or south to the tropics, or between Asia and North America.

But as you follow the corridor of time up the Red Deer River, probing into younger and younger rocks along the way, the diversity starts to decrease. Something was obviously going wrong. Dinosaur remains are much sparser in the sixty-five million-year-old rocks north of Drumheller, and evidence of only half a dozen species has been documented. Only the biggest or least specialized dinosaurs appear to have survived even this long. And finally, the rocks are silent except for the ghostly scurrying of small, furry creatures and the flurry of beating wings from the feathered descendants of the mighty dinosaurs – the birds.

It is here, in the thin layer of rock that marks the disappearance of the dinosaurs, that palaeontologists and geologists, chemists and physicists, astronomers and botanists, amateurs and professionals continue to probe, seeking the answer to one of the Earth's greatest mysteries. No other segment of geological time has been as thoroughly and consistently studied. Even so, we cannot explain what happened. We cannot ignore it either. It challenges our curiosity. We continue to search and study, to measure and compare and experiment. And, thankfully, we continue to imagine that ancient world.

It is a world captured brilliantly in *The Last Great Dinosaurs*. Monty Reid's text and Jan Sovak's art bring the great reptiles to life again, not only as enormous creatures that inspire our awe, but as animals that breathed, had babies, bled and hurt, fed and rested like the animals around us today. It is a colorful, lively book and as such, is a long-overdue tribute to the dinosaurs of the Alberta badlands. They were colorful, lively animals themselves, and this book does them justice.

– Philip Currie
Drumheller, Alberta
May 1990

The badlands of Alberta are a remarkable package of layered rock. Along the Red Deer River they are cut into a camouflage pattern of coulee and butte, of hoodoo and rill and fragmenting bone. They dissolve into field greys and khakis, broken horizontal lines of mud brown and a green with the heart leached out of it. It is as if they would constantly deflect attention away from their true outline, as if they were hiding something.

They are. They hide the remains of dinosaurs. These arid, scoured rocks are one of the most important sources of dinosaur fossils in the world. They record a time when the dinosaurs were at the height of their diversity, flourishing in an environment that must have seemed made for them. *Tyrannosaurus rex* stalked the era. Herds of horned dinosaurs swept across it. Duckbills, their newly hatched babies not much bigger than crows, grazed its lush vegetation. Armored dinosaurs, the graceful ornithomimids and small, vicious predators were all abundant. The world was theirs.

And then a thin, rather inconspicuous line. If looked for carefully, it can be seen in many parts of the world. In the badlands north of Drumheller, you can trace it for miles high in the valley walls. A careless footprint can cover it today, but it is the Earth's memory of a global disaster. It marks the end of the Cretaceous Period and was formed some 65 million years ago. Scientists know it as the Cretaceous-Tertiary Boundary. It is evidence of a changed environment, the edge of a new world. It was a world no dinosaur ever set foot in.

If one thinks of the Cretaceous-Tertiary Boundary as a fence around the dinosaurs' world, then the dinosaurs known from Alberta lived right beside the fence. There were a lot of them. The Alberta record speaks of a time when dinosaurs were in their last, great flowering. They had already dominated for millions of years. Many different species, including most of the giant sauropod planteaters, had appeared and died. As the last dinosaurs approached the Boundary, they were tremendously varied, increasingly big-brained, incipiently warm-blooded, at the peak of their success. For the last 10 million years of their reign, a time Alberta sediments document particularly well, they did not seem likely candidates for extinction.

And then, bigger than the biggest dinosaur, extinction showed up anyway. Its record is written clearly in the rocks. Below the thin, dark layer, dinosaur bones are plentiful. Above it there are none.

It is this combination of unprecedented success and complete annihilation that makes the dinosaurs of Alberta so significant and so fascinating. Although dinosaurs have been found on every continent, it is only in western North America that enough remains are preserved to allow analysis of the dinosaurs' last years. Alberta is one geographical focus for this analysis.

There is an intellectual focus as well. Few palaeontological debates are as durable as the one about what killed the dinosaurs. It intrigues researchers and has tremendous fascination for everyone else. Can we learn enough about the dinosaurs' demise to still anxieties about our own?

Nonetheless, researchers are turning their attention increasingly to what made the dinosaurs so successful. Perhaps this recent shift in emphasis reflects a sociological shift as well, from the fatalism of extinction to the numbed desperation to succeed. Dinosaurs have always borne this kind of cultural baggage. Alberta specimens are helping, increasingly, to carry the load.

This book is an introduction to those specimens. With simple language and many illustrations, it describes this province during the time of the dinosaurs. There are brief sections on where and how dinosaur fossils are found and where they can be seen now. Every kind of dinosaur found in Alberta is identified and described.

Not that there won't be changes. Like most dinosaur books, this one will contain misidentifications and wrong explanations. The extensive work conducted in Alberta in recent years increases the likelihood of new discoveries and new interpretations. Nonetheless, this book provides an up-to-date, accessible introduction to one of the world's most formidable faunas – the dinosaurs of Alberta.

INTRODUCING
DINOSAURS

What is a Dinosaur?

No one has ever seen a dinosaur. They've been dead for over 65 million years. Yet most of us have a good idea of what they looked like. They persist in our imaginations. They're in comics, on television, in movies and in museums. Few other animals fascinate us in the same way.

Today, dinosaurs are fossils. Bones, teeth, eggs and tracks are all that remain of these once abundant animals. People have known about these remains for hundreds of years. Only recently, however, have we begun to understand how the dinosaurs lived.

Dinosaur Diversity

Dinosaurs may be fossils today, but in the Mesozoic Era, 250–65 million years ago, they were living reptiles. They populated all parts of the world and adapted to many different environments. They likely roamed across the land where you now live.

The remains of hundreds of dinosaurs have been unearthed in Alberta's Dinosaur Provincial Park. In a single bonebed, the jumbled bones of more than 50 horned dinosaurs have been preserved.

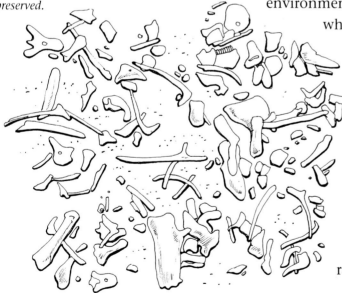

Dinosaurs first appeared about 230 million years ago. Their earliest undoubted remains come from South America. In Alberta, some dinosaur footprints are as old as 100 million years. Most of this province's dinosaur fossils, however, rarely date back more than 85 million years. Older rocks that might contain dinosaur remains are rarely exposed in the province.

Not all dinosaurs were big. Some were the size of crocodiles and others were no bigger than roosters. Some may have sported feathers. Many had other birdlike characteristics. Birds are in fact their closest living relatives.

Other dinosaurs were huge. Bone fragments found in the United States indicate one type of dinosaur may have been bigger than a blue whale, the largest living animal. This dinosaur, tentatively

The plod of giants, the scurry of runts, dinosaurs came in many shapes and sizes. Left to right: Spinosaurus, Kentrosaurus, Coelophysis.

known as *Seismosaurus,* may have weighed as much as 50 elephants. Large meateaters had fangs longer than a man's hand.

In between, they came in all shapes and sizes. They were just as different from each other as people are from monkeys, or cattle from camels. More than 340 different dinosaur species have been discovered, and more are likely to be found. They dominated the land as no other animals dominated it before or since.

And they lasted. We often think of them as failures, as dumb, slow-moving and extinct. But dinosaurs flourished for more than 150 million years. They were one of the most successful groups of animals ever.

Alberta sediments do not record the complete dinosaur story. They contain fossils primarily of the Cretaceous age, from 140 to 65 million years old. In fact, almost all of Alberta's dinosaurs come from the last part of the Cretaceous, a time referred to as the Late Cretaceous. Earlier chapters of dinosaur history are recorded elsewhere in the world, from the high Arctic to Australia. But the story in Alberta is a rich one. It records the dinosaurs at the peak of their success.

It was success that came after millions of years of development and change. Dinosaurs flourished only after life was well established on the Earth. They were not the earliest inhabitants of the planet. Many living things had gone before.

Prelude to the Dinosaurs

You can trace your ancestry back at least 3.5 billion years. So can everything else that lives on earth. Life itself is that old.

It began in the brew of the Earth's early seas. There, the first living cells, feeding upon complex chemicals known as proteins, began their evolutionary journey. The cells grew and divided and absorbed the proteins at an ever-increasing rate.

When the proteins became scarce, the cells evolved another method of feeding. They absorbed energy from sunlight and used it to manufacture organic material they could use as food. This process is known today as photo-synthesis. The cells in which it developed were the first green plants.

Simple, single cells began developing into something more complex about one and one-half billion years ago. Larger cells with a more complicated internal structure appeared. They developed the ability to clump together to form large multi-celled organisms with specialized cells for specific jobs. They evolved new methods of feeding, invented sex and are the fabric out of which all higher forms of life are made.

Multicelled creatures soon evolved into worms, jellyfish and other boneless animals, some of which have changed very little in the past 500 million years. Some began building hard body parts, a development that enhanced the fossil record tremendously, since it is hard parts, rather than the soft organs of the body, that are usually fossilized.

By 350 million years ago, life was well established on land. Insects, plants and amphibians had colonized the continents. Reptiles evolved from the amphibians some 290 million years ago. Like the amphibians, these early reptiles were low-slung and cold-blooded. But they had scaly, waterproof skin, modified lungs and hearts, and the ability to lay drought-resistant eggs on land. These adaptations enabled reptiles to occupy a full range of land environments.

Simple cells like these are known as prokaryotes. They can be found in volcanoes and icebergs, as well as almost everywhere else. They are the earliest known form of life.

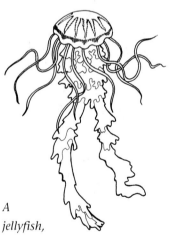

A jellyfish, an early and persistent organism, may be little more than well-organized water, but it is well adapted to its environment.

14

The Reach of Geological Time

Geological time is a wire the Earth runs into each and every one of us. It plugs into the chemicals and minerals that course through our bodies and claims them for the deep, prehistoric past. The same 19 elements out of which all life is made can also be found in the soil beneath our feet. We come, in a very literal way, out of the Earth.

Such claims have not always been easy for western cultures to acknowledge. We cannot, after all, recollect prehistory in any conventional sense. It cannot be remembered. There are no written records. Yet it lingers in our bones. And it lingers in the fossil record, the remains of living things that help us trace our links with the past and help us grasp the tremendous amount of time necessary for life as we know it to develop.

Scientists have devised the geological time scale to help comprehend the tremendous reach of the past. Based largely on our knowledge of rocks in the Earth's crust, the time scale is one of the most important tools we have in understanding the history of life. This time scale compresses 4.6 billion years into simplified form.

The Earth was already one billion years old when life first appeared. This was during the Precambrian Era, which stretched from Earth's first appearance to the development of complex organisms some 600 million years ago.

The Palaeozoic Era, 600–250 million years ago, was a time of rapid evolution. Most of the major groups of plants and animals that we are familiar with today made their first appearance.

Dinosaurs did not appear until the Mesozoic Era, 250–65 million year ago. Although they were a relatively late evolutionary development, they still preceded man by millions of years. The Mesozoic is divided into three periods: the Triassic, Jurassic and Cretaceous. Each has characteristic dinosaur remains.

The Cenozoic Era, 65 million years ago to the present, saw mammals flourish. The human species is a newcomer, having been on the scene in any recognizable form for only a few million years.

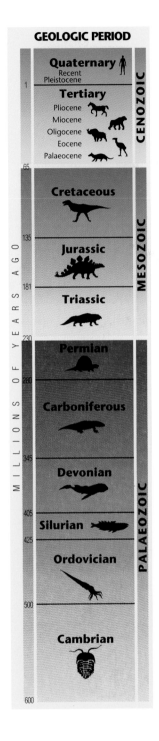

The geologic time scale is based on layers of rock. Each layer represents a different time. The oldest lies at the bottom, the youngest near the top. Most layers can be identified by characteristic fossils. Fossils used to define such layers, and hence different portions of geological time, are known as index fossils.

15

Major extinction events provide boundaries for many of the divisions of geological time. The dinosaurs, of course, disappeared at the end of the Mesozoic Era. An even more catastrophic extinction marks the end of Palaeozoic. Smaller-scale extinctions have been common throughout time. The boundaries mark crucial transitions from one system of life to another.

The time scale in the graphic represents an ideal based on what we currently know about the Earth's past. Although it is based upon rocks, one can rarely find a sequence of rocks that displays the entire range of time. Rocks and the fossils in them are studied around the world in order to devise the most precise order for time and living things.

Dinosaur Origins

Dinosaurs were reptiles. They first appeared some 230 million years ago. Their earliest representatives were small meateaters capable of running on their hind legs.

Dinosaurs lived on land. They didn't fly, like their relatives the pterosaurs. And they didn't live in the water. Plesiosaurs and ichthyosaurs were among the reptiles that had found ways to live in the seas, but they were not dinosaurs.

Reptiles were not the first to colonize the land. Plants and insects were ahead of them by millions of years. Large amphibians preceded them too. But the reptiles had features that made them particularly suitable for life in terrestrial environments. Most importantly, they produced tough-shelled eggs that did not dry out when laid in dry places.

As the reptiles spread across the land they diversified quickly. Some evolved a number of mammal-like characteristics. These mammal-like reptiles were highly successful, evolving more sophisticated teeth and jaws and better methods of controlling their body temperature. But they were not dinosaurs, and before they became extinct they gave rise to the true mammals.

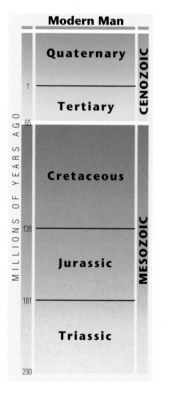

Mammals arrived on the scene early in the Mesozoic Era, birds and flowering plants somewhat later. Dinosaurs show up near the end of the Triassic Period, although large, mammal-like reptiles preceded them. The end of the Era is marked by the abrupt disappearance of the dinosaurs.

16

Mammal-like reptiles were surpassed by a still more successful group of reptiles. One branch of this line produced the snakes and lizards. Out of the other came the ARCHOSAURS, or 'ruling reptiles.' The archosaurs, some of which looked remarkably like modern crocodiles, first appeared more than 230 million years ago. Among them was a group of rapidly evolving and toothsome reptiles called THECODONTS. It was from the thecodonts that dinosaurs, along with flying reptiles and true crocodiles, evolved.

The thecodonts were a rearranged reptilian model. Changes in the hip and leg structure enabled them to use what is known as a variable gait. Most earlier reptiles were sprawlers. Their limbs protruded sideways from their bodies. The thecodonts could sprawl, but they could also draw their legs partially under their bodies, thus lifting their bellies off the ground and giving them a more upright stance.

This repositioning of the limbs, along with a modified ankle joint, gave the thecodonts better support and greater speed, and it eventually enabled them to lift their front limbs off the ground. At first they could do this for only short sprints, much like lizards do today. But dinosaurs soon developed a fully upright gait. The only other animals to do this were the birds and the line of mammals that gave rise to our species.

An upright gait was a clear advantage for dinosaurs. It provided additional thrust onto the ground and hence greater speed. This advantage assisted the dinosaurs in their rapid diversification. They soon overran most ecological niches, and by the end of the Triassic Period, 193 million years ago, dinosaurs were the dominant life on land.

Dimetrodon, a reptile but not a dinosaur, had a spine-supported sail along its back. The sail may have functioned as a solar panel, helping the animal to control its body temperature. Dimetrodon was a sharp-toothed carnivore that lived before the earliest dinosaurs.

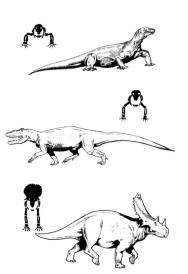

Most reptiles, like the varanid lizard (top), sprawl. Thecodonts like Euparkeria *(middle) stood more erect.* Chasmosaurus *(bottom) demonstrates the fully upright posture evolved by dinosaurs. Such changes helped to support increasing body size and allowed for greater variety of movement.*

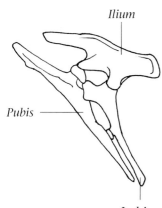

Ornithischian pelvis

Ilium

Pubis

Ischium

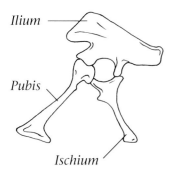

Saurischian pelvis

Ilium

Pubis

Ischium

Why did two basic hip structures evolve in dinosaurs? No one is certain, but they may have grown out of a need for increased locomotion. In fast-moving, long-striding dinosaurs, the pubis would have to stay out of the way of the thigh and would have been better positioned close to the ischium. Dinosaurs that needed to support greater bulk, like the large sauropods, retained the forward-thrust pubis.

A Sense of Order

For many years, dinosaurs were viewed as a single group of reptiles. But in 1887, only three years after the first well-documented dinosaur find in Alberta, scientists classified dinosaurs into two major, distinct lineages. They are defined most readily by the shape of their pelvic bones, although other less obvious characteristics are also important.

The first dinosaur order to evolve was the SAURISCHIAN, or 'lizard-hipped' group. The largest land animal ever to live, take your pick among *Brachiosaurus, Supersaurus, Seismosaurus* or *Mamenchisaurus,* and the undisputed largest terrestrial carnivore, *Tyrannosaurus rex,* were both saurischians.

Late in the Cretaceous, however, they were outnumbered by the second major order of dinosaurs, the ORNITHISCHIANS. Ornithischians had birdlike hips. Some walked on their hind legs, while others went around on all fours. All of them ate plants, and all of them possessed a small bone at the front of the jaw, the predentary. A useful feeding tool, the predentary is one of the trademarks of the ornithischians.

Like the saurischians, the ornithischians came in a multiplicity of shapes. Some had tail clubs, others armored plates. They came with crests, frills and horns. In Alberta, the horned dinosaurs were particularly abundant.

Naming Names

Dinosaurs have complicated names. They're often Latin and frequently hard to pronounce. They are part of a system developed in the 18th century, one that is used to classify all living organisms.

Dinosaurs have two-part names. The first is known as the genus name, the second part as the species name. We often use two-part names in everyday conversation. People in our society are frequently known by two names. For example, Dennis Johnson is clearly a member of the Johnson family, with his light complexion, wiry build and receding hairline. However, we can readily tell him apart from his brother Wilmer, who has equally thin but darker hair and the same build. Dinosaur names work in a similar way. They point to similarities and to differences at the same time.

In general terms, this is how a dinosaur gets classified.

We know dinosaurs are animals,
so they belong to the kingdom ANIMALIA.

Dinosaurs all had backbones,
so they belong to the phylum CHORDATA.

All dinosaurs were part of the class REPTILIA.

There are two main orders of dinosaurs,
ORNITHISCHIAN and SAURISCHIAN.

Skeletal reconstruction of Albertosaurus Sternbergi, the dinosaur discovered near Drumheller by C. H. Sternberg.

This one had lizardlike hips,
so it belongs to the order SAURISCHIA.

Massive head and distinctive hand and foot structure identify this dinosaur as part of the TYRANNOSAUR family.

First discovered in Alberta,
this dinosaur was given the genus name ALBERTOSAURUS.

This dinosaur was discovered by C. H. Sternberg,
thus its common name is ALBERTOSAURUS STERNBERGI.

Before the Boundary
Alberta in the Late Cretaceous

Dinosaurs dominated the Mesozoic Era, 250–65 million years ago. Their remains found in Alberta, however, come from only a small segment of that time, from about 80–65 million years ago. Although dinosaurs lived in Alberta earlier, a few footprints are the only surviving record of their presence from that time. Earlier sediments are buried deep beneath the plains or folded high into the mountains.

The Alberta frequented by the dinosaurs was much different than the Alberta we know today. The world in general was cooling but was still warmer than at present. Oceans were contracting, but the North American interior was still flooded by a shallow sea.

At its greatest extent, the sea linked the Gulf of Mexico and the Arctic Ocean. Its shoreline was unstable. Sharks teeth and the remains of marine reptiles have been found in the sediments of Dinosaur Provincial Park, indicating that some sea-going creatures could have made their way up rivers into the deltaic areas. And for a significant part of the Late Cretaceous, the sea actually inundated the Park. In all, the marine influence must have been substantial. The seasons were less marked and, in general, the climate more equable.

At the continent's western margin, the Rocky Mountains were being thrust upward. Microcontinents and arcs of volcanic islands, pushed by the motors of continental drift, had collided with the North American landmass. The coastline crumpled. A network of rivers spilled down the flanks of the newly formed mountains, washing their sediments to the ocean and, to the east, the interior sea. A flat coastal plain buffered the mountains from the sea, and across it the rivers dug their channels. As they reached the sea, they fanned out across huge deltas. Humid and warm, the deltas supported a rich variety of life.

Cordillera
Inland Sea

For much of the Late Cretaceous, a shallow sea lay across the interior of North America, linking northern waters to those of the Gulf of Mexico. The land mass to the west, called Cordillera, had been gradually built up as island chains accumulated. The island sediments, uplifted and eroded, eventually were carried by rivers to the inland basin, where they once again became the bottom of a sea.

20

Fed by sediments from the uplands, fertile soils developed, and a lush plant growth commandeered their richness. Their remains are preserved as leaf imprints, fossil wood and, most importantly, pollen. Flowering plants, a recent evolutionary innovation, were plentiful. Magnolia, oak and tupelo trees were scattered among redwood groves. Swamps draped with cypress fronds and luxurious ferns, destined to become seams of coal in the walls of the Red Deer River valley, sweated in poorly drained areas. Notably absent, however, were grasses, which did not appear until the Cenozoic.

Sharing the dinosaurs' world were other reptiles, fishes, and mammals. The remains of turtles, some with shells bigger than the lids of garbage cans, have been found in the Alberta badlands. Birds and flying reptiles shared air space with winged insects. It was a rich and complex ecosystem.

Conditions were ideal for dinosaurs. Even in the Arctic, where tundra and foreboding icepack are the norm today, frost was unusual. The Arctic climate then was similar to Vancouver's today. In spite of the long, polar night, dinosaurs made their homes in the high latitudes as well.

It was in this equable environment that the last dinosaurs lived. They lived on the uplands and in the swamps. They were plentiful and varied, and although a few kinds, such as *Triceratops*, seem to have been increasingly dominant, their evolutionary potential was still considerable. They could have, according to evidence available from most Late Cretaceous rocks, survived.

The remainder of this book will provide a closer look at every genera of dinosaurs known from Late Cretaceous Alberta.

Today, the nearest sea is hundreds of kilometers from Alberta. Prairies, mountains and forests now dominate the province. In all of Alberta's ecosytems, the remains of ancient life can be found. The fossils of tiny marine animals have lifted high into the Rocky Mountains. Dinosaur bones lie buried the plains.

IDENTIFYING
DINOSAURS

The
Hadrosaurs

The Hadrosaurs
Duckbill Dinosaurs

The hadrosaurs, or duckbill dinosaurs, were the most abundant dinosaurs in Alberta in the Late Cretaceous. They are one of the dinosaur families about which we know the most.

Their remains have been found in many parts of the world, including Europe and South America. China and Mongolia have been sources of many specimens, some of which are remarkably similar to those found in Alberta.

Hadrosaurs probably descended from a dinosaur similar to *Camptosaurus*, a planteater that roamed North America during the Jurassic Period. *Camptosaurus* had short, strong forelimbs and a thick neck. Its hands had five fingers, whereas hadrosaurs only had four.

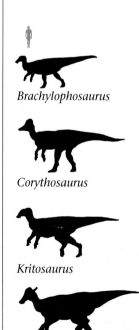

Alberta Hadrosaur Localities

Brachylophosaurus

Maiasaura

Hypacrosaurus

Corythosaurus

Parasaurolophus

Edmontosaurus

Kritosaurus

Prosaurolophus

Anatosaurus

Lambeosaurus

Saurolophus

Gryposaurus

26

Among the earliest known hadrosaurs is *Bactrosaurus*, which seems to have evolved in China 100 million years ago. Sturdily built, this planteater was some six meters (17 ft) long. Although poorly known, its skeleton appears to be like that of other duckbills. Hadrosaur teeth of a similar age have been found in England and other countries. Not long afterward, the duckbills show up in North America.

Clearly designed for movement on land, hadrosaurs wandered through lowland forests, cropping tough vegetation with the ducklike beaks that give them their popular name. They probably walked on their hind legs with ease – their hind limbs were twice the size of their forelimbs. Many hadroasurs were the size of elephants. Although they all had similar body builds, many had distinctive head crests.

Corythosaurus *skin had a pebbled surface, similar to that of a football. The surface on the belly was smoother than that of the back. Different hadrosaurs had different skin patterns, perhaps suggesting different coloration.*

Dinosaur tracks found in the Peace River Canyon in British Columbia indicate the presence of hadrosaur-like reptiles some 120 million years ago. Most other hadrosaurs come from a later time.

140   120   100   80   65

MILLIONS OF YEARS AGO

Living Together
Life Among the Hadrosaurs

For the hadrosaurs, blessed with few natural defenses, survival was a matter of living together. The ability to live as a community was undoubtedly an important factor in their remarkable success.

Evidence for community life comes from several sources. Hadrosaur nesting sites, which contain eggs, unhatched babies and the remains of juveniles, have been discovered in a number of places. A remarkable 1987 discovery at Devil's Coulee in southern Alberta disclosed a dinosaur rookery, where the bones of baby dinosaurs have been found in abundance. The nests appear to have been built in exposed locations and were probably protected by adults. Adults may have brought food to the nests until the young were ready to forage for themselves. Certainly the nests attracted the attentions of predatory dinosaurs, whose teeth have been found among the baby bones.

Duckbills may have been noisy animals. Their head crests, of which an amazing variety are preserved, probably functioned as resonating chambers to help the animal bawl and honk. Top to bottom: Corythosaurus, Lambeosaurus, Parasaurolophus.

28

Hadrosaurs had acute sight and hearing, and many hadrosaur skulls show an unusually large nasal cavity, suggesting that the living animals possessed a keen sense of smell as well. This may have given them early warning of any predator.

When alarmed, hadrosaurs may have trumpeted a warning to the rest of the herd, which may have splashed into nearby water. Or they may have scattered into the forests, where their colors blended with the surrounding vegetation.

Adaptability was a major factor in the hadrosaur success story. They lived in most parts of the world. Their remains have been unearthed north of the Arctic Circle and as far south as Patagonia. Recent evidence suggests they may have migrated seasonally, like modern caribou.

The passage of the herd. Like salmon crowding a mountain stream or buffalo on the vanished plain, a duckbill herd tramples through a narrow corridor toward its wintering ground.

Although duckbills spent most of their time on land, they could probably swim when necessary. Some predators may have been able to pursue them into the water.

29

Alberta Hadrosaurs

Alberta is the richest area in the world for hadrosaur remains. They were first identified in 1881, when Richard McConnell found a duckbill's thighbone in pieces in a coulee near Nobleford. Fragmented bones had been found even earlier along the Milk River, but they had not been properly described. Since then, many specimens have been recovered from locations ranging from Grande Prairie to Manyberries.

Among the Alberta hadrosaurs, a striking separation seems to exist between coastal forms and upland forms. Similar distinctions are seen in the ceratopsians as well.

Brachylophosaurus
short crest lizard

This rare duckbill was first discovered by Charles M. Sternberg in 1936 in a sandstone ridge above the Red Deer River near Dinosaur Provincial Park. At first, Sternberg thought it belonged to a known species, but its long forelimbs, heavy skeleton and small crest marked it as distinct. *Brachylophosaurus* probably lived in forests, where it browsed on leaves and flowering plants. At about seven meters (20 ft) in length, it was longer than an average pickup truck.

*A*n ominous shadow closes in on a striped Brachylophosaurus *as it makes its way across a floodplain. No evidence exists to demonstrate what color dinosaurs were, but most scientists think they would have looked something akin to living reptiles. While many contemporary reptiles prefer greens and browns and other conservative pigments, some are spectacularly colored. Some dinosaurs may have been as well.*

Corythosaurus
helmet lizard

Corythosaurus had a tall, rounded crest on top of its narrow head. To its discoverer, Barnum Brown, the crest looked like the helmet of a gladiator. *Corythosaurus* grew to about 10 meters (31 ft) in length, about as long as a boxcar. But it was more graceful. It had a long, flexible neck, a narrow back and a long tail useful for balance when it stood upright. This is one of the best-known dinosaurs. Many specimens have been unearthed in Alberta, some with extensive skin impressions preserved along with the bones.

Surprised by an opossum patrol, two young *Corythosaurus* seek shelter among their mother's legs. Confrontations like this were probably common in the Late Cretaceous. Mammals and dinosaurs evolved at about the same time, although mammals remained small and inconspicuous throughout much of the dinosaurs' reign. By the Late Cretaceous, however, mammals were evolving into larger and increasingly varied forms.

Kritosaurus
chosen lizard

Kritosaurus is named for its prominent nasal bone, which looks to some like a Roman nose. Other than the humped nose, *Kritosaurus* had a relatively flat head. It was about 10 meters (31 ft) long and weighed more than four tonnes (4.5 tons).

Known from New Mexico, Wyoming and many other locations, *Kritosaurus* seems to have preferred life on the well-drained basins and plains to life in the swamp. Its remains were first found in Alberta by George F. Sternberg, who discovered a well-preserved skull and partial skeleton along the Red Deer River in 1913. Some researchers consider *Kritosaurus* to be the same as *Hadrosaurus,* but not everyone agrees.

*A*fter a storm
has passed,
Kritosaurus *browses ferns
and mosses along an
eroded gully in Late
Cretaceous Alberta. The
rich vegetation has left
its thumbprint in the
fossil record in many
ways, most
importantly as spores
and pollen. Tough and
tiny, these reproductive
bodies enable us to identify
many kinds of ancient plants
and thus help to determine
what prehistoric
environments were like.
Alberta in the Late
Cretaceous was milder and
more humid than it is today.*

Lambeosaurus
Lambe's lizard

Named in honor of Lawrence Lambe, who discovered its partial remains in 1898 near Berry Creek, *Lambeosaurus* was the first crested duckbill found in North America. Since then, other remains have been found in the Alberta badlands and also near Manyberries. *Lambeosaurus'* crest was a prominent blade and spike combination; like many other hadrosaur crests, it was hollow and varied in size according to age and sex. Although most specimens are about 10 meters (31 ft) long, some recent discoveries suggest it may have reached 15 meters (46.5 ft), making it the largest crested duckbill known.

Dawn light seeps through drooping branches as a group of lambeosaurs drinks at a stream in Late Cretaceous forest. This pose is based on the drinking pose of the lambeosaurs at the Royal Tyrrell Museum of Palaeontology in Drumheller.

Maiasaura
maternal lizard

Maiasaura was first found in Montana, but fragmentary remains have been discovered in southern Alberta. It was about nine meters (28 ft) long and had a tiny knob between its eyes. Its nose holes were unusually small for a hadrosaur. It was called maternal lizard because its Montana remains were found near nests containing the remains of babies. This is the only dinosaur with a feminine name.

Evidence suggests that *Maiasaura* provided some care for its young. Their nests, each about two meters (six ft) in diameter, were lined with vegetation. Hatchlings were about the size of crows and seem to have stuck close to their nests, where parents may have brought food to them. Even the nest-bound hatchlings have some wear on their teeth, perhaps a result of chewing the regurgitated meal a foraging adult dispensed. Some scientists think the young may have remained in the nest for up to two months.

Maiasaura *spreads a cover of sand over her newly laid eggs. She will then place a layer of plant material over the eggs as well. As the vegetation rots, it will keep the eggs warm. The nest itself is a hollowed-out mound of mud placed not far away from other nests of the colony. Australian Mound Birds build similar nests today. The eggs, about the size of cantaloupes, were probably laid near the end of the dry season so that the young would emerge during the rainy period.*

Parasaurolophus
beside ridge lizard

This unusual hadrosaur is rarer than most other duckbills. Skin impressions are preserved along with it, and three of the ribs had been broken during life. Most remarkable of all is the hollow, trombonelike crest that sweeps backward from the skull. This was once thought to have functioned as a snorkel but is more likely to have been used for dinosaur orchestration. Recent studies indicate that *Parasaurolophus*, like *Kritosaurus*, preferred to live in more open, upland areas. *Parasaurolophus* was about nine meters (28 ft) long and weighed up to four tonnes (3.5 tons).

A freak snowstorm
sweeps across a pair of
Parasaurolophus, *whose long*
crests are among the most
bizarre of any dinosaur's.
Although cold-blooded
dinosaurs would not have
survived prolonged winter
conditions, they undoubtedly
lived through less than
ideal weather occasionally.
This may have been
particularly true for
those dinosaurs living
in the high latitudes,
as some duckbills did.

Prosaurolophus
before ridge lizard

Prosaurolophus is the earliest known Alberta hadrosaur with a solid crest. It was probably an ancestor to *Saurolophus*. *Prosaurolophus* had a broad snout, but its bill was smaller and shorter than many other hadrosaurs. It had a small crest that ended in a short spike. It was about 15 meters (48 ft) long, among the biggest hadrosaurs anywhere. Barnum Brown discovered *Prosaurolophus* in 1915 in what is now Dinosaur Provincial Park.

*B*edding down for the night, Prosaurolophus settles among the undergrowth at the edge of a Late Cretaceous forest. Like most large animals, duckbills probably spent much of their time either sleeping or eating.

Saurolophus
ridge lizard

A solid ridge running along its snout and ending in a spike at the top of its skull is the distinguishing feature of *Saurolophus*. It lived in North America and Asia and grew to lengths of 14 meters (45 ft), although most Alberta specimens are considerably smaller. Discovered by Barnum Brown in rippled-marked sandstone near the site of the Tolman Bridge in 1911, this was the first complete dinosaur to be found in Canada. The find helped spark the great dinosaur rush in the early part of this century.

Up on its hind legs and under full power, Saurolophus *flees* across a dried-out plain before an advancing tornado. Although about the size of an elephant, hadrosaurs weighed less and were more graceful and agile. When necessary, they could move quickly, with their powerful hind legs propelling them across open country or through water.

Hypacrosaurus
high-ridge lizard

One of the most robust Alberta hadrosaurs and possibly a descendent of *Corythosaurus, Hypacrosaurus* had a thicker crest but was otherwise very similar to its predecessor. This planteater probably browsed on the undergrowth in humid forests but rarely ventured into the swamps. It had a high-ridged back, which may have acted as a radiator, helping to regulate the animal's internal temperature. Known primarily from Alberta, *Hypacrosaurus* remains were first discovered by Barnum Brown near Tolman Ferry in 1912. Several different kinds of closely related hypacrosaurs may have lived in Alberta.

Nests found at Devil's Coulee were made by a *Hypacrosaurus*-like dinosaur. The eggs, about the size of cantaloupes, seem to have been laid herringbone-fashion in long rows and may have been covered with sand and plant material. Australian Mound Birds build similar nests today.

*T*he lush, algae-thickened swamp provides a rich meal for two young Hypacrosaurus, *but it also threatens to make a meal of them. Lurking in the water is* Leidyosuchus, *a 4-meter (13-ft) long crocodile.* Leidyosuchus *was among the reptiles that survived the extinctions at the Cretaceous-Tertiary Boundary, although it disappeared soon afterwards.*

Edmontosaurus
Edmonton lizard

Edmontosaurus was probably the largest hadrosaur to live in Alberta and may have been one of the most abundant. It probably reached lengths of 15 meters (48 ft). Its uncrested, no-nonsense skull was about the size of a horse's head. It had a high-ridged back and may also have possessed balloonlike flaps of facial skin, which may have inflated as the animal bellowed. Such flaps, perhaps brightly colored, may have functioned as sexual signals during mating season.

Recent statistical surveys indicate that *Edmontosaurus* was particularly abundant in the damp lowlands near the shore of the inland sea. *Edmontosaurus* remains were first discovered in 1912 along the Red Deer River valley west of Munson.

Plowing through the mud of a river delta, an Edmontosaurus rouses flocks of pterosaurs. A Quetzalcoatlus, with a wingspan up to 15 meters (48 ft), the biggest flying animal ever, has swept a fish from the shallow water. In the background, smaller Pteranodons *sail on the offshore wind. Most pterosaur remains have been found in marine sediments, but the living animals likely inhabited other areas as well.*

Anatosaurus
duck lizard

Anatosaurus is among the best-known dinosaurs. It had a long skull containing more than 1000 teeth and ending in a wide ducklike bill. It lacked a head crest. One *Anatosaurus* specimen has been discovered with its stomach contents fossilized, showing that it had eaten the needles of pine trees. It had a heavy tail and a mitt of skin covering its fingers. This was one of the most primitive members of the hadrosaur family, but it was also one of the last to be around.

The Anatosaurus herd moves out in the early morning mist along a riverbank in Late Cretaceous Alberta. Massive finds in Montana, one containing remains of some 10,000 animals, indicate that duckbills lived in large herds. Herding behavior was an important defensive strategy for the duckbills, just as it is for some large mammals today.

Gryposaurus
hook-nosed lizard

First discovered by George Sternberg in 1913 and named by Lawrence Lambe the following year, *Gryposaurus* was a particularly well-preserved find, with an unbroken skull and skin impressions among its features.

Like most hadrosaurs, *Gryposaurus* was an elephant-sized planteater. Webbed front feet suggest it was comfortable in swampy environments. Its most notable characteristic is a large hump over the nostrils. But it also possessed a bill with an unusually crinkled edge, which may have helped the animal filter plant material from the water. *Gryposaurus* seems to have disappeared before the mass extinctions at the Cretaceous-Tertiary Boundary.

*A*lert to movement along the opposite bank of a stream, a Gryposaurus searches the mist for any other dangers. Solitary hadrosaurs would have been more vulnerable to attack than a large herd was. Even so, it would have required a concerted effort for most predators to bring down an animal as large as a hadrosaur.

The
Pachycephalosaurs

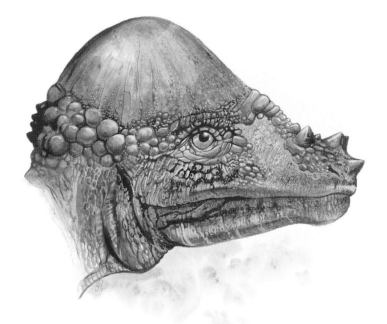

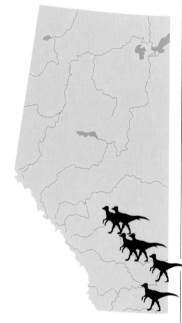

Alberta Pachycephalosaur Localities

The Pachycephalosaurs
Thick-Headed Dinosaurs

The pachycephalosaurs, or thick-headed dinosaurs, were an unusual dinosaur family. The bones of their high-rise skulls could be as thick as a loaf of bread. The brain inside the skull, however, was no bigger than an average doughnut hole.

Lighter and smaller than the duckbills, the pachycephalosaurs had short forelimbs and small, sharp teeth. Their eyes were relatively large, and they probably had a good sense of smell. They walked on their hind legs, although they may have dropped to all fours as they rooted for plants.

Pachycephalosaurs are not a well-known dinosaur family. Their skeletons are rare, but fragments of the skullcap are often discovered. They are solid pieces of bone, not easily eroded and probably not favored by predators.

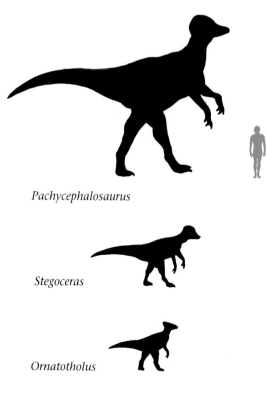

Pachycephalosaurus

Stegoceras

Ornatotholus

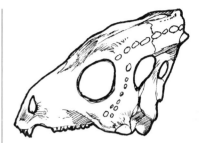

The skull of Ornatotholus, *shown here without a lower jaw, lacked the pronounced thickening found in other pachycephalosaur skulls. The small teeth near the back of its mouth were used for shredding plant material.*

They may have been carried by rivers and streams for great distances. They were certainly in the water for a long time. A single, partial skeleton, collected in 1921, is known from Alberta. More complete specimens, some of them almost identical to Alberta pachycephalosaurs, have been found in Mongolia. An unusual type is known from Madagascar.

Pachycephalosaurs probably developed from a bipedal dinosaur like *Hypsilophodon*. This plant-eating dinosaur was compact but agile, moving through the Mesozoic world with the grace of an antelope.

The earliest known pachycephalosaur was found on the Isle of Wight. A small part of it, an incomplete skull, was discovered in rocks some 125 million years old, whereas all of the specimens found in Alberta are much younger. Not much bigger than a turkey, *Yaverlandia* probably had short front limbs and a long, stiff tail. Two patches of thickened bone above the eye sockets mark it as an early pachycephalosaur.

Pachycephalosaurs likely rooted for tubers and insects with their front feet.

57

The skull of Pachycephalosaurus shows not only the thick skullcap but the studs and knobs on the rear of the skull and the snout. These were probably ornamental growths.

Most pachycephalosaurs were fairly small by dinosaur standards. They possessed good vision and a keen sense of smell, and if a predator approached, the pachycephalosaurs probably galloped away, tails held stiffly out behind them.

For many years, pachycephalosaurs were thought to have lived in small groups in upland areas, away from the hustle and bustle of the coastal plains. Today some evidence, including a a partial skeleton and other finds in Dinosaur Provincial Park, suggests that thick-headed dinosaurs inhabited lowland areas as well.

Like many animals that live in herds, pachycephalosaur males may have engaged in combat to establish dominance and attract mates. Mobile battering rams, they likely butted heads like bighorn sheep.

Some scientists think they may have hit each other in the ribs rather than head-on, since the latter may have been particularly dangerous.

In a particularly interesting calculation, zoologist R. McNeill Alexander calculated that a pachycephalosaur weighing 20 kilograms (50 lbs) running at three meters (10 ft) per second would impact a solid object with almost a tonne (1.1 ton) of force.

While the skull may have been thick enough to absorb such a shock, the rest of the body would have had to have some flexibility, or it would have broken up on impact. Alexander proposes that the neck of pachycephalosaurs may have acted as a crumple zone that would temporarily deform to absorb the shock and then straighten out again.

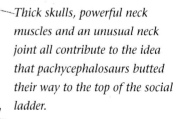

Thick skulls, powerful neck muscles and an unusual neck joint all contribute to the idea that pachycephalosaurs butted their way to the top of the social ladder.

140   120   100   80   65

MILLIONS OF YEARS AGO

Alberta Pachycephalosaurs

Three different kinds of thick-headed dinosaurs have been found in Alberta. A fourth kind, identified as *Gravitholus*, is known from a partial skullcap unearthed near Jenner. Although it has been given the name *Gravitholus,* it may in fact belong to a juvenile *Pachycephalosaurus*.

Stegoceras
horny roof

Stegoceras males had smooth, rounded domes about as thick as two of these books stacked on top of each other. The females probably had thinner domes. On both, a fringe of bony studs protruded from the back of the skull. Their brains were large by pachycephalosaur standards.

About the size of a five-year-old and with a tail almost as long as its body, this dinosaur probably lived on uplands where the Rocky Mountains are today, although its remains have been found in low-lying areas as well. It is the most common pachycephalosaur in western Canada. *Stegoceras* remains were first discovered by Lawrence Lambe in Alberta in 1898. Similar specimens are known from Mongolia and China.

*W*hile the rest of the herd watches from the shadows, two large Stegoceras *males battle for dominance in a cycad-lined clearing. The ornate ring of bones around the skull may have served as a visual signal to warn off most challengers, but dominant males would still have to fight off younger individuals from time to time.*

Ornatotholus
ornate dome

Knobs adorning its somewhat thickened skull gave this dinosaur its name in 1981. It lacked the high dome possessed by other pachyrhinosaurs. The top of its skull, although thick, was flat. Instead of butting heads, males may have engaged in head-to-head shoving matches. It was similar in size to *Stegoceras*. Until *Ornatotholus* was discovered in Alberta, the only other flat-headed dinosaurs came from Mongolia and China.

Ornatotholus
did not have the
greatly
thickened
skullcap
most other
pachycephalosaurs
possessed. However,
it did have the
decorative knobs
and studs common to
the family. Males and
females may have had
different coloration, although
there is no way of proving
this through the fossil
record. Nor is there any
way of determining the
relative size of males
and females.

Pachycephalosaurus
thick-headed lizard

This dinosaur grew to about seven meters (22 ft) long, the largest known member of the family. It also had the thickest skull. Knobs and spikes cobbled its snout and ringed the back of its skull. It was a planteater and had short, sharp teeth. It appeared late in the Cretaceous and survived longer than the other pachycephalosaurs. A huge skullcap collected in Dinosaur Provincial Park in 1916 is the first fossil from this animal collected in Alberta.

Its tail held rigidly behind it, Pachycephalosaurus trots across a parched mudflat. As big as many of the hadrosaurs, Pachycephalosaurus was a solidly built animal. It had studs not only on the back of its skull but along its snout as well. Mud cracks and ripple marks are sometimes preserved in Late Cretaceous rock, evidence of the dinosaurs' environment.

© J. SOVAK
1990

The Hypsilophodonts

Alberta Hypsilophodont Localities

This illustration is based upon a sketch by Neave Parker, who pictured hypsilophodonts as tree dwellers. This was an idea suggested by initial research on hypsilophodont material, but further studies disproved the notion.

The Hypsilophodonts
Ridge-Toothed Reptiles

Hypsilophodonts were quick-moving bipedal planteaters. Fast runners, they had long but sturdy hind limbs with long toes. Their necks were neither as long nor as slim as those of the ornithomimids, but their tails were long and supported by a latticework of tendons. The tendons enabled the hypsilophodonts to hold their tails out behind them as they ran, giving them better balance. Most had stubby, five-fingered hands and slightly longer four-toed feet.

They take their name, which means "high-ridged tooth," from their distinctive teeth.

Thescelosaurus

Parksosaurus

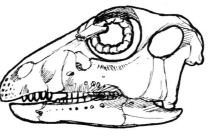

The bony ring around the eye of this hypsilophodont may have helped to focus the animal's vision. Muscles to operate the jaw passed through the opening behind the eye socket.

Hypsilophodonts did not make nests like the hadrosaurs did, although they both may have covered their eggs with plant material. An important hypsilophodont nesting area has been found in Montana. Remains of embryonic dinosaurs were curled in many of the eggs.

Most hypsilophodonts had two types of teeth in their jaws. At the front were sharp, cone-shaped teeth, while further back in the jaws lay broader, blunter teeth more typical of planteaters. Their jaws were solidly built. Cheek pouches held food as it was being chewed.

The largest hypsilophodont was probably about five meters (16 ft) long, but most were no more than three meters (10 ft). From their first appearance to their final extinction at the end of the Cretaceous, they changed very little in basic shape.

For many years, the earliest known hypsilophodont came from Jurassic rocks some 150 million years old. It was found on the Isle of Wight in 1849. More recent finds in China indicate hypsilophodonts flourished there at the same time. Other Jurassic specimens come from North America and Africa. Hypsilophodonts seem to have spread to many parts of the world; recent finds suggest they inhabited Australia and Antarctica as well.

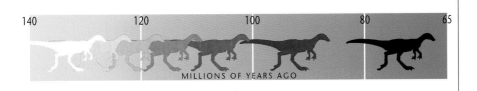

140   120   100   80   65

MILLIONS OF YEARS AGO

69

Alberta Hypsilophodonts

Most researchers think two hypsilophodonts are known from Alberta, although some argue that one, *Thescelosaurus*, belongs in its own family. They seem to have lived along the many streams that coursed through Late Cretaceous Alberta.

Thescelosaurus
pretty lizard

C. M. Sternberg first collected *Thescelosaurus* in the badlands west of Rumsey in 1926. Sternberg's find was in rock layers of Late Cretaceous age, near the Cretaceous-Tertiary Boundary, indicating that *Thescelosaurus* may have been one of the last dinosaurs. It was certainly the last known hypsilophodont.

Yet it shares the characteristics of hypsilophodonts from 50 million years earlier. It had the same basic body plan, with a long, stiff tail and and a solid torso. It may have been bulkier than its forerunners, and its thigh was longer than its calf, an unusual situation for a hypsilophodont. Small teeth sat in the front of its mouth, while high-ridged teeth were positioned further back in its jaws.

Recently, *Thescelosaurus* teeth have been found in Dinosaur Provincial Park. The teeth are found in localities that suggest *Thescelosaurus* preferred inland environments, away from the damp, near-shore areas.

A one-time marsh burns, and four long-thighed Thescelosaurus dash before the flames. After the fire would come the new growth, and the dinosaurs would return to crop the fresh vegetation. Hypsilophodonts were among the most durable of dinosaur families. They survived, in one form or another, for some 100 million years.

Parksosaurus
Parks' lizard

Parksosaurus was a big-eyed, long-legged planteater. At some 2.5 meters (eight ft) in length, it was slightly smaller than *Thescelosaurus*. Its teeth were slightly different as well in lacking the high ridge characteristic of other hypsilophodonts.

Parksosaurus was found by a University of Toronto expedition in the Red Deer River badlands near Rumsey in 1922. The left half of the skeleton was preserved, but the rest of the bones had long since disappeared. What remained of the skull had been flattened. It was named after William A. Parks, one of Canada's early palaeontologists, who was in the party that collected it.

In a deciduous forest beside a stream that frets its way into a ravine, the unusual Parksosaurus feeds on the waxy leaves of an ivy. Fossil pollen and spores, preserved in abundance in the sediments, give evidence that bald cypress and palmettos flourished among the elm, ash and magnolia trees.

The
Ornithomimids

Alberta Ornithomimid Localities

The Ornithomimids
Bird-Mimic Dinosaurs

With long legs, long tails and long, flexible necks, these small, graceful dinosaurs remind many people of emus and ostriches. In fact, their name, ornithomimids, means bird mimics.

As with many dinosaur families, their early history is poorly known. The ornithomimids appear in the middle of the Cretaceous and survive until its end. It is thought they evolved from Late Jurassic ancestors known from 160 million-year-old deposits in Africa.

The later ornithomimids could sprint rapidly across the open ground and were probably the most agile of dinosaurs found in Alberta. Their feet were clearly built for rapid movement, with long toes and even longer bones in the upper foot. The similarity to the structure of an ostrich foot is striking. The construction of the pelvis allowed for a rapid leg swing, additional evidence for great speed.

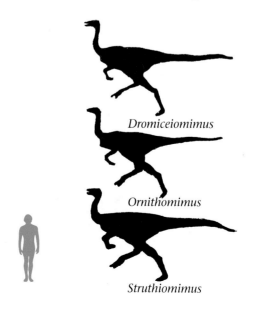

Dromiceiomimus

Ornithomimus

Struthiomimus

76

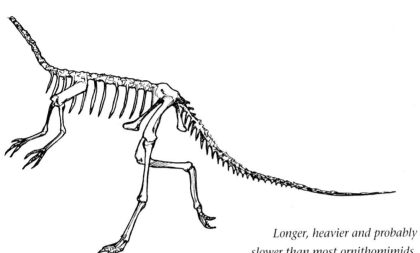

The similarities between ostriches and ornithomimids *are striking. About the same size, they had similar builds and probably lived in similar ways.*

Longer, heavier and probably slower than most ornithomimids, Elaphrosaurus *may nonetheless be a close relative. It was discovered by German fossil hunters in East Africa early this century. Although its skeleton is well preserved, no skull has ever been found.*

Many of their bones were hollow. The skull was paper thin, but it enclosed a relatively large brain. These dinosaurs are often considered the most intelligent reptiles of their time, although their increased brainpower was probably used to control their reflexes and balance.

Ornithomimids had small, lightly built heads with toothless beaks and unusually large eyes. Their front limbs were long and ended in three spindly fingers, each with a relatively straight claw longer than a grizzly bear's. Like ostriches, the ornithomimids were probably omnivorous and may have used their fingers to rake the ground cover for small mammals and lizards or to pull fruit from trees.

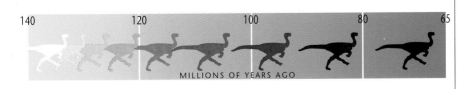

140   120   100   80   65

MILLIONS OF YEARS AGO

Other theories have suggested that these dinosaurs ripped open anthills or stepped through shallow water, spearing crabs and other invertebrates. The first is unlikely because ornithomimids lacked the strong shoulder muscles necessary to dig for food. The second remains a possibility.

Their toothless beaks, while not equipped for tearing prey apart, enabled the ornithomimids to eat a wide variety of food. They were capable of grasping small objects such as fruit or eggs. Fish, insects, mammals and lizards may have been on their menu as well. The influential palaeontologist Barnum Brown suggested that they ate shellfish, fishing them raccoon-style from the water.

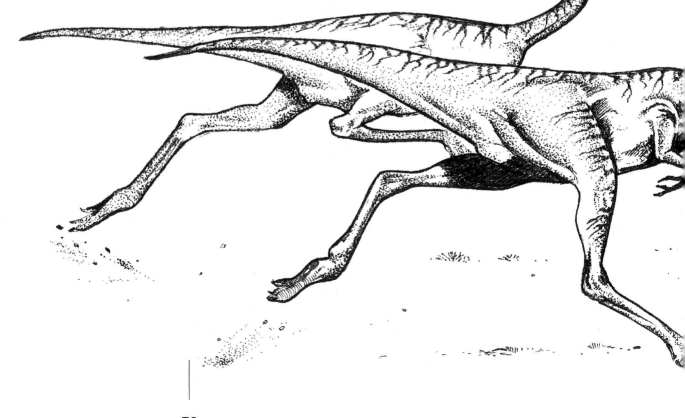

Ornithomimids may have cared for their young to some extent. The adults had an unusually wide pelvic canal, giving rise to the unproven suggestion that live young were borne. Perhaps these dinosaurs simply laid large eggs.

Although many meat-eating dinosaurs grew much larger, the ornithomimids were obviously a successful group. They were initially described in the United States in 1890. Since then, their remains have been found in many parts of the world, including Africa, Asia and North America. Important specimens have been found in Alberta, with fragmentary remains coming from as far north as the Swan Hills.

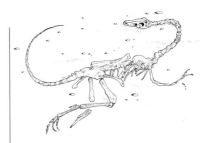

Many ornithomimid skeletons are found in this position, with their necks and tails dramatically curved. Once thought to be the result of strychnine poisoning, it is now known to be caused by the stiffening of muscles in the tail and neck after death.

Ornithomimids were fast company. With their long tails held rigidly behind them, they cruised the plains of Late Cretaceous Alberta. Few dinosaurs could match them for speed, although dromaeosaur packs may have caught them occasionally.

Alberta Ornithomimids

Three different ornithomimids are known from Alberta. Their remains, including North America's best-known specimens, are especially common in the Late Cretaceous sediments of Dinosaur Provincial Park. At the time, a large inland sea covered much of western Canada. The bird-mimic dinosaurs ranged along its shores and onto the neighboring uplands. Their bones are found in what were once evergreen forests west of the ancient sea.

Dromiceiomimus
emu mimic

This dinosaur had the largest eyes of any known land animal. It may have hunted at twilight, flushing mammals and lizards from the underbrush and snatching them with its supple, three-fingered hands. It could probably run faster than an ostrich but couldn't manoeuvre as quickly. Its legs were slightly longer than the other ornithomimids, and its back was probably a bit shorter. Its total length was about three meters (10 ft).

Its brain was about the size of an ostrich brain, suggesting that this dinosaur may have been intelligent enough to provide care for its young. An adult specimen has been found buried with two juveniles in strata high on the east bank of the Red Deer River.

D romiceiomimus young learn a necessary trade, as a parent teaches them how to snatch fish from the water. Lush green ferns flourish beneath a canopy of redwoods in the Late Cretaceous lowlands not far from the present location of Drumheller, Alberta.

Ornithomimus
bird mimic

Ornithomimus darted through the swamps and forests, preying on frogs and salamanders, bending down the boughs of trees to strip their leaves, and rooting for eggs and tubers. Its large eyes could detect approaching predators effectively, and its strong hind legs could carry it rapidly to safety.

About four meters (13 ft) long and lightly built, these dinosaurs ranged across much of Alberta. Their remains were first discovered in this province in 1916 by G. F. Sternberg. Since then, important specimens have been found in Dinosaur Provincial Park and near Trochu. Scattered remains and a tail are known from Sandy Point on the South Saskatchewan River.

Flushed from beneath a decaying redwood log, a small lizard attempts to scuttle from the jaws of an adult Ornithomimus. A spindly fingered young dinosaur looks on. Pale mushrooms climb from the murk of the forest floor, while overhead hang the fronds of a cycad.

Struthiomimus
ostrich mimic

Struthiomimus was stronger and heavier than the other
ornithomimids found in Alberta, although its overall length
was about the same as *Ornithomimus*. It inhabited the open
country along riverbanks. The claws on its feet were flattened,
probably to provide additional traction. It was toothless, but
the jaw may have been covered with a beaklike sheath.

The first *Struthiomimus* remains in Alberta were found in
1901 by Lawrence Lambe. A few years later an almost complete
skeleton was discovered by Barnum Brown in what is now
Dinosaur Provincial Park.

In a Late Cretaceous chase scene, a Struthiomimus carries off a lobster, one of the many marine creatures that inhabited Alberta in the Late Cretaceous. Another Struthiomimus gives pursuit. Footprints of these dinosaurs have been preserved in sandy sediments laid down near ancient bayous.

The
Oviraptors

Alberta Oviraptor Localities

The Oviraptors
Egg-Stealing Lizards

The oviraptors, or egg-stealing lizards, aren't well known. Although their fragmented remains turn up in Dinosaur Provincial Park and elsewhere, the pieces are tiny and scattered, and piecing together one of these small dinosaurs is an uncertain procedure. Speculation about their behavior is risky as well.

The first discovery of *Oviraptor* came in 1923, when an American expedition to Mongolia found the bones of a small, apparently predatory dinosaur lying above a clutch of fossilized eggs. The predator had a toothless beak, long forelimbs and a skull similar to a bird's. In addition, it had a collarbone much like the wishbone in modern birds, an extremely unusual arrangement for a dinosaur.

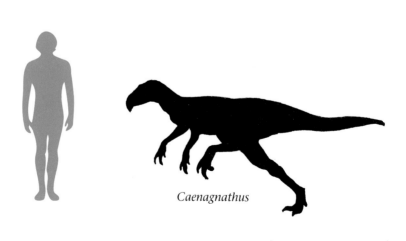

Caenagnathus

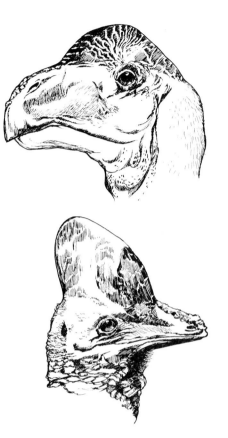

Short, toothless and lightweight, the skull of Oviraptor philoceratops *from Mongolia (above left) is something of an oddity. It bore a large head crest, much like today's* cassowary *(left).*

In spite of these features, the specimen was clearly a dinosaur, not a bird. And it probably didn't live by eating eggs. Its hard beak and curved jaws were powerful, capable of crushing molluscs and small bones. Its three-fingered hands could have carried prey to its mouth. Its claws, however, were not large, and its tail lacked the stiffeners often found on other small carnivores. The oviraptors probably weren't as dependent upon their tails for balance.

Built along the same graceful lines as the ornithomimids, the oviraptors grew to about two meters (six ft) in length. They first appeared about 80 million years ago.

140   120   100   80   65

MILLIONS OF YEARS AGO

An Alberta Oviraptor

Although the remains of small meat-eating dinosaurs are among the most sought-after specimens, they continue to be rare. Few oviraptor specimens have been found in Alberta sediments.

Caenagnathus
recent jawless

Caenagnathus is the only Alberta dinosaur thought to belong to the oviraptor family. Although its name suggests it had no jaws, it did. In fact, the jaws were the only part of the specimen preserved. A Sternberg expedition found the first specimens in a cliffside quarry some 40 meters (125 ft) above the Red Deer River in 1936.

These jaws were toothless and birdlike, and when *Caenagnathus* was given its first scientific description four years after the initial discovery, it was described as a bird. One of the compelling pieces of evidence for this description was the presence of a wishbone, thought only to be found in birds. It was not until scientists realized that this specimen had features similar to oviraptors found in Mongolia that *Caenagnathus* was accepted as a dinosaur.

An estimated two meters (six ft) long, this dinosaur walked on its long hind legs. It was probably a swift runner, able to pounce on small reptiles and mammals. It prowled the deltas of Alberta some 74 million years ago.

Racing the incoming tide and competition from the airborne pterosaurs, a teal-headed Caenagnathus *zeroes in on the carcass of a primitive shark, beached on the shore of the inland sea that covered the western interior of North America for much of the Late Cretaceous.*

©
1990
J. SOVAK

The
Elmisaurs

Alberta Elmisaur Localities

The Elmisaurs
Foot Lizards

Relatively rare as fossils, the elmisaurs have been difficult to classify. They are best known from hands and feet discovered by Polish scientists working in Mongolia and from similar specimens found in Alberta. Their name comes from a combination of the Mongol word for foot with the Greek word for lizard.

Chirostenotes was first collected in Alberta in 1914, when G. F. Sternberg collected its slender hand bones in the badlands along the Red Deer River. Later on, a heavier foot was discovered and given the name *Macrophalangia*, or "big toes." An animal recently found in Alberta combines the hands of *Chirostenotes* and the feet of *Macrophalangia* into a single specimen, an elmisaur.

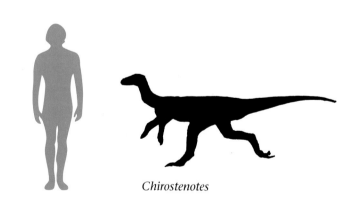

Chirostenotes

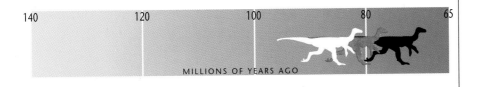

Elmisaurs had slim hands (bottom) but heavier feet. Each foot (top) had four toes, making it unlike the ornithomimids but more akin to other small theropods.

Lightly built meateaters, these dinosaurs probably stood about one meter (three ft) high at the hip. What distinguishes them from other small carnivores are their particularly long, three-fingered hands and heavily built feet, in which some of the bones have been fused together, a trait once thought to be found only in birds. Each foot had four toes, making it unlike the ornithomimids but more akin to other small theropods.

140 120 100 80 65

MILLIONS OF YEARS AGO

An Alberta Elmisaur

Few elmisaur remains are known from Alberta. Additional fragments may belong to this animal as well, but they cannot be precisely identified. Dinosaur names and relationships are often revised as new specimens are discovered and studied. This is particularly true of the small carnivores, which are often known only from partial skeletons.

Chirostenotes
narrow hand

This poorly known dinosaur was first collected in Alberta in 1914, when G. F. Sternberg collected its slender hand bones in the badlands along the Red Deer River.

Chirostenotes had long hands ending in sharp, curved claws. Compared with its hands, its feet were large and heavy. Although its skull has never been found, a lower jaw and a few teeth found some distance from the hands have been ascribed to this animal. The sharp, slightly curved teeth clearly indicate it was a meateater.

*L*unch *for a* Chirostenotes *family group was no first come, first served affair. A careful hierarchy likely prevailed in the pack, as it does in those of many animals. Here, a dominant adult scavenges the carcass of a juvenile hadrosaur while younger animals wait their turn. And in the wings, a ring-tailed marsupial patiently watches for the leftovers.*

The Dromaeosaurs

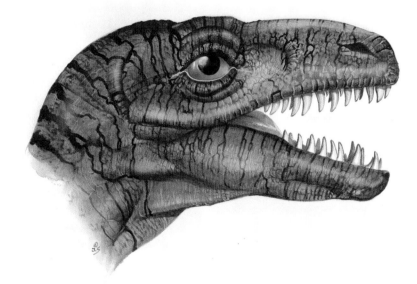

Alberta Dromaeosaur Localities

Dromaeosaurs
Running Lizards

Dromaeosaurs take their name from the Greek words meaning running lizard. Although they were likely agile animals, their legs were relatively short, and they may not have been particularly swift runners. But they were clearly active dinosaurs, with long, stiffened tails to act as stabilizers as they ran and a large brain to keep everything coordinated.

They were probably savage predators, and huge slashing claws on the second toe of each foot gave them fearsome weapons. The claws could have easily disembowelled other small dinosaurs. The specialized claws were so big they were held off the ground as the dromaeosaurs ran. Special muscles gave the dromaeosaurs a powerful, slashing kick as well.

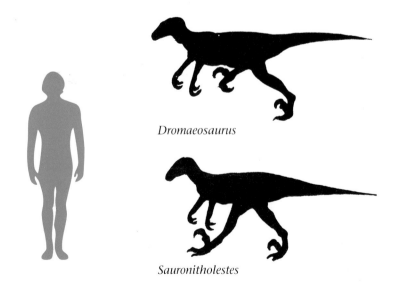

Dromaeosaurus

Sauronitholestes

100

Grim reaper of the Cretaceous, the sickle-shaped toe of Dromaeosaurus *had enlarged joints that enabled it to be held off the ground as the animal ran. It could also be swung in a wide and deadly arc. The rest of the foot provided sturdy support.*

Their teeth were small but sharp and capable of ripping through tough flesh. Sharp claws waited at the end of their three-fingered hands, and their upper arms were well developed, probably to help the animal hold on to resisting prey.

Smaller, older coelosaurs probably gave rise to these fast, fierce hunters, which were among the most important carnivores to evolve in the Late Cretaceous. There is evidence they hunted in packs, and a dromaeosaur patrol across the wetlands would have sent most animals scurrying for cover.

140   120   100   80   65

MILLIONS OF YEARS AGO

101

Alberta Dromaeosaurs

Compared with some of the other small carnivores from Alberta, dromaeosaurs are relatively well known. Enough material has been discovered to reconstruct the skeletons in a fairly precise manner. Comparisons with related specimens found in Mongolia and the United States have aided in the study of Alberta dromaeosaurs.

Dromaeosaurus
running lizard

The first of the dromaeosaurs to be discovered, *Dromaeosaurus,* was about the size of a large dog. Its jaws were long and solidly built for its size, and its neck was curved and flexible. It may have been able to smell its prey, and it probably possessed a good sense of hearing. Its tail was sheathed in a lattice of bony rods but was flexible at the base, allowing it to be carried in a sharply upturned aerial-like position. Its remarkably large eyes gave it excellent vision. Its vicious sicklelike claws, although shorter than those of other dromaeosaurs, still gave it a distinct advantage over most of its prey.

The first and only good *Dromaeosaurus* remains were found by Barnum Brown on the south bank of the Red Deer River in 1914. Several later discoveries disclosed *Dromaeosaurus* teeth among the bones of much larger dinosaurs. This led to speculation that dromaeosaurs attacked larger animals, but the teeth may simply have washed into the site. *Dromaeosaurus* seems to have become extinct about 70 million years ago, well before the Cretaceous-Tertiary Boundary.

Lightning strikes on a dusty plain, a Dromaeosaurus pack closes mercilessly on a scattering group of lizards. With tails carried like flags and slashing claws at the ready, dromaeosaurs were efficient predators. They probably cleaned up the kills of larger carnivores as well. For many years they were confused with the tyrannosaurs, and even today they appear to be scaled-down versions of the larger meateaters.

Saurornitholestes
bird robber

Saurornitholestes is the smallest adult dinosaur known from Alberta. Its remains were discovered in Dinosaur Provincial Park in 1974 by a park visitor who found teeth, parts of the skull and other bones in buff-colored sandstone high above the valley floor. Although the specimen is far from complete, enough material was unearthed to indicate the presence of a new kind of dinosaur, which was named in 1978.

Some two meters (six ft) long, *Saurornitholestes* was lighter and smaller than many of its carnivorous contemporaries. Its sense of smell was poorly developed, but it did possess the large brain typical of these agile dinosaurs. It had small, saw-edged teeth, and its claws were sharp and curved.

Cat-agile, Saurornitholestes lunges after a large, winged insect. Insects appeared long before the dinosaurs and reached their apex in the Carboniferous Period, some 300 million years ago. As the Cretaceous Period progressed, seasons became increasingly marked. Insects and plants adapted readily to this change. In this scene, deciduous trees are losing their leaves with the onset of cooler weather.

The
Troodons

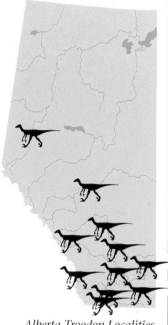

Alberta Troodon Localities

The Troodons
Wounding-Tooth Dinosaurs

The troodons take their name from the Greek words for "wounding tooth." For many years, their almost triangular, serrated teeth were the only evidence of this dinosaur family.

Troodon itself got its name in 1856, making it one of the first dinosaurs to be named in North America. The name referred to a single tooth found in Montana. For many years, scientists were uncertain about what kind of dinosaur it was. The troodons have been classified with pachycephalosaurs, hypsilophodonts and dromaeosaurs, among others. A recent find near the Royal Tyrrell Museum of Palaeontology in Drumheller seems to have clarified the situation enough to consider troodons as a distinct family. Important finds have also been made in China and Mongolia.

Troodons had similarities with other small carnivorous dinosaurs. Their teeth, small and pointed, are the teeth of a meateater. But their long, narrow and rather unusual hands, ending in thin, supple fingers, are unlike those of other carnivores.

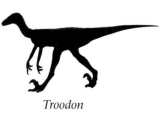

Troodon

Troodons had efficient flesh-cutting teeth. They were first thought to have come from a meat-eating lizard.

As with the dromaeosaurs, the troodons had a sicklelike claw on the second toe of each foot. Troodons, however, had longer lower limb bones, suggesting they were faster runners. They also possessed particularly large eyes, giving rise to the suggestion that they hunted at twilight. The eyes provided better depth perception than did those of most dinosaurs.

The bones of troodons are riddled with air spaces, or pneumatopores. The spaces reduce the weight of the bone and, since they are connected with the lungs, assist in respiration. Birds are the only living animals with similar air spaces.

140   120   100   80   65

MILLIONS OF YEARS AGO

An Alberta Troodon

Alberta was home to a number of highly evolved dinosaurs as the Cretaceous Period drew to a close. Many of them, although poorly known, were probably closely related.

Troodon
wounding tooth

Troodon was a large-brained, birdlike dinosaur. Smaller than an ostrich, it had long legs, a long tail and a relatively long neck. An energetic hunter, with sickle claws and sharp reflexes, it may have attacked small mammals when they were most active, after sunset. Its large eyes gave it excellent vision. Its tail was probably used as a high-speed stabilizer. Its three-fingered hands had opposable digits, enabling it to grasp prey firmly. Some scientists have called *Troodon* a "Cretaceous coyote."

Known from a partial skeleton, several skulls and other scattered remains, troodons are among the best known of the small carnivorous dinosaurs in Alberta.

Baffled by the disappearing act of the large soft-shelled turtle, Aspideretes, Troodon begins a closer inspection. The fragmentary remains of these turtles are often found in the Alberta badlands. Some Cretaceous turtles grew up to four meters (13 ft) in length. Aspideretes was smaller but no less interesting *for* Troodon.

The
Tyrannosaurs

Alberta Tyrannosaur Localities

The Tyrannosaurs
Tyrant Lizards

Big, bipedal and deadly, the tyrant lizards, or tyrannosaurs, were the largest meat-eating animals of all time. They were relative latecomers, appearing only a few million years before the great extinctions at the Cretaceous-Tertiary Boundary. But while they were here, they ruled. Their remains are well known from North America and Asia, with an unusual specimen coming from India. Only the largest horned dinosaurs may have been a match for these archetypal predators.

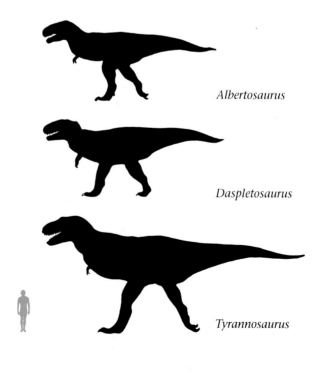

Albertosaurus

Daspletosaurus

Tyrannosaurus

The family tree of large carnivorous dinosaurs is open to several interpretations. Many scientists think that *Teratesaurus* was the first family of heavyset meateaters. As they evolved, they grew even larger in size, culminating in the giant *tyrannosaurus rex*. However, as their overall body size grew, their forelimbs failed to keep pace. These small limbs became less and less useful and gradually, over time, possessed fewer fingers. *Tyrannosaurus rex* had only two on each hand.

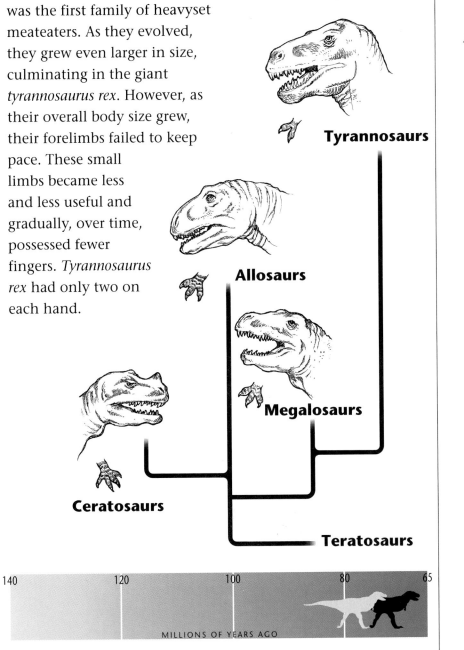

Tyrannosaurs

Allosaurs

Megalosaurs

Ceratosaurs

Teratosaurs

140   120   100   80   65

MILLIONS OF YEARS AGO

115

An Albertosaurus *skull was a robust meat-eating mechanism. Its teeth are sharp and curved and set in solid jaws. Windowlike openings reduce the weight somewhat but not as much as in earlier carnivores such as* Allosaurus.

As heavy as elephants, tyrannosaurs had massive skulls, some of which were longer than a human leg. Their brains occupied only a small portion of the skull but were still relatively large when compared with those of other dinosaurs. Their jaws were powerful and lined with sharp, serrated fangs. A short, sturdy neck supported the big head. Their hind limbs were powerful, but their two-fingered front limbs were short and puny, unable even to reach their mouths. Only the largest horned dinosaurs may have been a match for these archetypal predators.

They were clearly meateaters, and they probably hunted their prey, although they would have scavenged for food as well. Their jaws could have inflicted mortal wounds on the largest of planteaters.

Like many carnivores, tyrannosaurs may have been fiercely territorial. For the loser of such a dispute, death was a distinct possibility.

Although the large tyrannosaurs were big animals, they could probably move quickly when necessary. Their hind limbs were long and their pelvis surprisingly narrow. Even with their huge size, the skeletons of tyrannosaurs are birdlike in many ways.

Tracks preserved in the canyon of the Narraway River in northeastern British Columbia show the heavy footprints of an *Albertosaurus*-like carnivore. There is no evidence of its tail dragging through the mud, so we think tyrannosaurs probably walked with their tails held stiffly out behind them. This would have been necessary to counterbalance the weight of the skull in any case.

Although he was surveying for coal, J. B. Tyrrell knew he had found a dinosaur when he saw a great skull leering at him from the rocks of the Red Deer River valley. Although his collecting techniques weren't very sophisticated, Tyrrell was able to ship the skull back to Ottawa for further study.

Tyrannosaur tracks have been preserved in several places in Alberta, as well as in other locations in western North America.

Alberta Tyrannosaurs

Three different kinds of tyrannosaurs could be found in Alberta during the Late Cretaceous. They hunted on the deltas and in the forests, ambushing ceratopsians and duckbills, and scavenging food wherever they could. Their bones are fairly common in Alberta, although complete skeletons are rare. In the declining dinosaur populations near the Cretaceous-Tertiary Boundary, tyrannosaurs were the only large predators found in Alberta.

Albertosaurus
Alberta lizard

Albertosaurus bones were among the earliest dinosaur remains collected in Alberta. A skull found by J. B. Tyrrell in 1884 was the first important dinosaur fossil to be discovered along the Red Deer River. It was named in 1905, the same year that Alberta became a province. Since then, many *Albertosaurus* fossils have been discovered. The smallest documented *Albertosaurus*, a juvenile less than a quarter of the size of a full-grown adult, was collected from Sandy Point on the South Saskatchewan River in 1986.

Almost 10 meters (31 ft) long, *Albertosaurus* was the most common of the large carnivores in Late Cretaceous Alberta. It had long, sharp teeth and sharp claws on its hind feet. Its limbs were slightly longer than the other tyrannosaurs, so it was probably the fastest member of the family and may have chased down duckbills. It appeared in North America before *T. rex* but lasted right to the end of the Cretaceous.

Large carnivores were probably opportunistic eaters. Here, in a marsh at the edge of an inland sea, a mud-caked Albertosaurus spies the carcass of a short-necked plesiosaur. Although sea-dwelling reptiles, plesiosaurs may have swum up rivers to lay their eggs. Their bones have been found in river sediments in Dinosaur Provincial Park.

Daspletosaurus
frightful lizard

Although *Daspletosaurus* lived at the same time as *Albertosaurus,* it wasn't as plentiful. Like other tyrannosaurs, it had daggerlike teeth and powerful hind legs. It was smaller than *Tyrannosaurus rex* but had more teeth, and its forelimbs were stronger than all the other tyrannosaurs. *Daspletosaurus* inhabited the marshlands common in Alberta 68 million years ago. Its remains were first found by C. M. Sternberg near Steveville in 1921, although they weren't identified until later. Some scientists think *T. rex* and *Daspletosaurus* may be the same thing.

A

placid

scene

belies the

power and

speed of

Daspletosaurus,

resting in

the cool

undergrowth

after a meal.

Honeysuckle vines

dangle from the

forest canopy and

recently evolved

flowers spill down

toward the stream. In

the water drift

indifferent sturgeon,

almost indistinguishable

from their modern descendants.

Tyrannosaurus
tyrant lizard

Tyrannosaurus was one of the last dinosaurs to live in Alberta. The largest known meateater, it was more than 12 meters (37 ft) long and stood almost as tall as a giraffe. Unlike a giraffe, however, *Tyrannosaurus rex* was massive and powerful.

Its skull in particular was an imposing unit of bone. Up to 60 teeth, some of them longer than a human hand, lined its jaws. If humans had been around, they could have slid down its gullet with ease. Its eyes faced forward, providing better depth perception, important for a predatory animal, and its narrowed snout gave it a clear field of vision. At the other end, a heavy tail counterbalanced the skull. A complete tail has never been found, so no one knows exactly how long it might have grown. *T. rex* is one of the most famous of the extinct reptiles.

Two good *Tyrannosaurus rex* specimens are known from Alberta. One was collected from the Crowsnest Pass area in 1982. The other, found near Huxley in the Red Deer River valley, was without a skull. It can be seen on display at the Royal Tyrrell Museum of Palaeontology at Drumheller, with a cast skull taken from a specimen at the American Museum of Natural History.

*P*estered by a trio of dromaeosaurs, Tyrannosaurus rex protects its meal of a young horned dinosaur. T. rex was one of the few animals that may have been able to bring down a feisty ceratopsian successfully. The distinct three-toed tracks of the giant trail away across the coastal dunes. Similar tracks have been preserved in many places in Alberta.

The
Ceratopsians

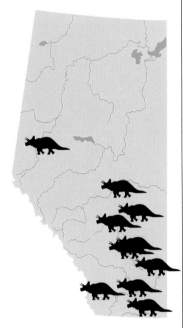

Alberta Ceratopsian Localities

The Ceratopsians
Horned Dinosaurs

The horned dinosaurs, or ceratopsians, were the last major group of dinosaurs to evolve. In the latter part of the Cretaceous, they underwent rapid evolution and many different forms appeared. Most of them were heavy, four-legged planteaters with powerful jaws that ended in parrotlike beaks. Sporting a variety of frills and horns, large ceratopsian herds probably trundled across North America as the Age of Dinosaurs came to a close.

More than 18 ceratopsian species have been discovered in North America. In Alberta, 14 different species have been identified. Most of them have been found along the Red Deer River.

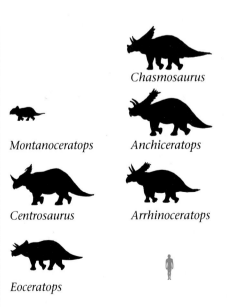

Chasmosaurus

Pachyrhinosaurus

Montanoceratops

Anchiceratops

Styracosaurus

Centrosaurus

Arrhinoceratops

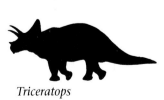

Triceratops

Eoceratops

Early ceratopsians appeared at about the same time as the first flowering plants. Perhaps their sharp beaks and powerful skulls helped them utilize this new food source.

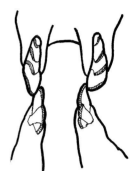

Ceratopsian teeth worked like scissors, shearing plant material into bite-sized lengths. Teeth of the upper jaw fit over their couterparts in the lower jaw.

The earliest known ceratopsian is *Psittacosaurus*. About the size of a big dog, it had a large head with the distinctive parrotlike beak that is one of the defining features of the ceratopsians. *Psittacosaurus* is well known from skeletons found in China and Mongolia. One such skeleton is that of a baby about the size of a chipmunk, one of the smallest dinosaurs ever found.

A more advanced ceratopsian, *Protoceratops,* was about the size of a pig. It was a four-legged creature with a short body but a relatively large head. It had a beak and a large frill with two holes in it. All known *Protoceratops* fossils have been found in China and Mongolia. None of the large, later horned dinosaurs have been found in China.

Another primitive-looking ceratopsian, *Leptoceratops,* lived in what is now Alberta. It was lighter than *Protoceratops* and probably better suited to running. It had a short, solid crest. Although it had primitive characteristics, it coexisted with much later, better known ceratopsians. Its teeth are some of the latest known dinosaur fossils.

Ceratopsians had banks of teeth set in their jaws. Worn-out teeth were replaced by new teeth throughout the animal's life.

127

More than 70 Protoceratops eggs were discovered in Mongolia in 1922. The females probably scooped out hollows for the nests, laid the pineapple-sized eggs and covered them with sand.

Larger beaks, jaws and frills made the skull heavy, and it is possible that ceratopsians reverted to a four-legged stance in order to support the increased head load better. As the animals grew larger and could no longer hide or flee with ease, horns may have developed as a means of defence and intimidation. The horns may also have functioned, along with the frill, as part of a sexual display. Both males and females had horns.

Like most dinosaurs, ceratopsians hatched from eggs. The young may have been cared for by the parents until they were old enough to join the herd. When travelling, young ceratopsians probably remained at the center of the herd for protection.

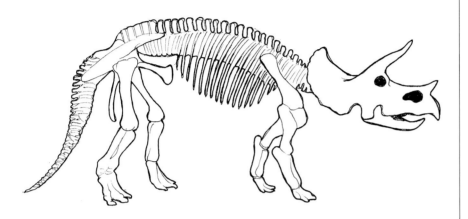

Ceratopsians had such big heads that their necks had to be specially reinforced to support the weight. The pelvis and shoulder were both sturdy, and the tail was so short it barely touched the ground.

Huge dinosaur graveyards provide provocative indications that ceratopsians travelled in herds. The jumbled bones in such bonebeds are often from a single species, and sometimes include dinosaurs of all ages, suggesting that a large herd may have perished together.

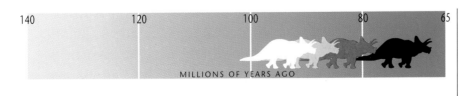

One ceratopsian bonebed in Dinosaur Provincial Park is larger than a hockey rink. It contains the remains of at least 50 horned dinosaurs. Many similar bonebeds have been found in the Park.

140   120   100   80   65

MILLIONS OF YEARS AGO

129

Alberta Ceratopsians

Ceratopsians are divided into two groups. Short-frilled ceratopsians had frills that did not reach their shoulders, whereas long-frilled varieties had, obviously enough, longer frills. Both kinds have been found in Alberta, as have the remains of a protoceratopsian, a kind of ceratopsian throwback.

Although some scientists think that the large, horned dinosaurs preferred open, drier areas, recent interpretations argue that some large ceratopsians were swamp dwellers. There may in fact have been distinct swamp and upland communities, each featuring characteristic dinosaurs, and these differences may have become more pronounced late in Cretaceous times, perhaps in response to climatic changes. Regardless of where they made their homes, ceratopsians were among the most abundant dinosaurs in North America late in the Cretaceous Period.

Montanoceratops
horn face from Montana

This small, horned dinosaur was among the primitive ceratopsians knowns as protoceratopsians. They possessed the bony frill and the parrotlike beak typical of the ceratopsians, but their horns were poorly developed. Protoceratopsians were as a rule smaller than the ceratopsians too.

Montanoceratops is best known from discoveries made in Montana by Barnum Brown. Remains have been found in Alberta as well, both in Dinosaur Provincial Park and in the Crowsnest Pass area. Although it possessed many primitive characteristics, *Montanoceratops* was a Late Cretaceous dinosaur, sharing the uplands with more advanced forms such as *Styracosaurus*. About as long as a motorcycle, *Montanoceratops* had a high, flexible tail and heavyweight head.

Caught in the falling snow in the uplands of what is now the Crowsnest Pass area of Alberta, Montanoceratops follows its stubby horn through the night. It is late in the Cretaceous and winters are becoming increasingly cool. Leaves have been swept from the deciduous forest. It is a night better suited to the fur-covered mammals, but even they have taken shelter.

Centrosaurus
sharp point lizard

The remains of this dinosaur were first noted in Alberta by palaeontologist Lawrence Lambe in 1904. Even today, most of the known remains come from the badlands of the Red Deer River.

Probably the same as *Monoclonius, Centrosaurus* grew up to six meters (19 ft) in length. Its skull alone was more than one meter (three ft) long, with a single forward-thrust nasal horn and small growths over each eye. Bony growths decorated the edge of its frill, and protective tongues of bone drooped over the two large frill openings. Some specimens have been discovered with skin impressions.

With ghostly moss-draped cypresses in the background, a solitary Centrosaurus *makes its way across the swampy lowlands of what is now Dinosaur Provincial Park. A flurry of birds lifts from the rushes before it. Bird bones are extremely light, often hollow and are rarely preserved as fossils.*

Pachyrhinosaurus
thick-nosed lizard

Pachyrhinosaurus grew to about six meters (19 ft) in length, making it one of the larger horned dinosaurs.

Small knobs grew on its brow, and its frill was edged with short spikes, but for many years it was thought to be hornless. Instead, it had a rough mass of bone about as thick as a car tire on its snout. Although some researchers suggested that the bony pad may have been the base of a horn or the scar left where a large horn had been broken, very little additional information could be garnered from the original specimen collected by Charles M. Sternberg near Big Valley in 1946.

More recently, however, pachyrhinosaur remains have been identified at Scabby Butte in southern Alberta and in the late 1980s, the Royal Tyrrell Museum of Palaeontology excavated a pachyrhinosaur bonebed near Grande Prairie. Specimens there, more than 2,200 bones in all, have provided new insight into the pachyrhinosaurs. It now seems likely that two different species inhabited the province. Other pachyrhinosaur remains have been found as far north as Alaska.

134

*A*t home in a cypress swamp, a Pachyrhinosaurus *from the deltas of southern Alberta overturns a stump. Bigger than the ceratopsians known from the older sediments of Dinosaur Provincial Park,* Pachyrhinosaurus *had power to spare for this kind of activity. Its unusual array of horns may have had a defensive function but was more likely ornamental.*

Styracosaurus
spiked lizard

Styracosaurus had six long spikes jutting from its frill, small horns above its eyes and a nasal horn almost as long as a baseball bat, giving the animal a profoundly spiny appearance. Slightly smaller than *Centrosaurus*, it is built to the same body plan. C. H. Sternberg discovered the first *Styracosaurus* remains in 1913 near the old settlement of Steveville in the Red Deer River valley.

*S*unlight glints on the the spikes and frills of Styracosaurus *adults as they drive a pack of dromaeosaurs from more vulnerable quarry, the young ceratopsian. Formidable and mobile, styracosaurs probably formed a defensive pocket into which the young scrambled. Individual adults would charge attackers in an attempt to drive them off, much as musk-oxen do today.*

© J. SOVAK
1990

Chasmosaurus
opened lizard

This horned dinosaur is named for the large openings, or chasms, in its frill. One of the most common ceratopsians of its time, *Chasmosaurus* had a small nose horn and two larger horns on its brows. Its skin was made up of buttonlike scales, impressions of which were found along with a skeleton near Steveville along the Red Deer River in 1913. At slightly more than five meters (16 ft) in length, the sturdily built *Chasmosaurus* was smaller than its later relatives and may have been the ancestor of the other long-frilled ceratopsians. It is also known from Texas.

Shielding a yearling from a spectacular lightning storm, a Chasmosaurus *family seeks shelter. One of the common horned dinosaurs that inhabited the deltas in what is now Dinosaur Provincial Park,* Chasmosaurus *is a typical long-frilled ceratopsian. It is also the earliest known long-frilled genus.*

©J. SOVAK
'90

Anchiceratops
close horned face

Anchiceratops had three horns, a stubby one on its nose and longer ones over its eyes. Its thin, bony frill, scalloped around the edge, had relatively small openings and stretched back over its shoulders. It is similar to but slightly bigger than its earlier relative, *Chasmosaurus*. Most of its remains have been found near coal-bearing sediments, suggesting that this dinosaur lived near marshy areas. The first known *Anchiceratops* fossils were discovered by Barnum Brown along the Red Deer River in 1911.

*T*hree Anchiceratops *dip into a pond lined with lily pads to cool off on a hot day. While the young relax, the adult surveys the undergrowth for possible danger. Screw pines shade the animals. The rich vegetation of the swamp is preserved as seams of coal in the walls of the Red Deer River valley near Drumheller.*

Eoceratops
dawn horned face

First described in 1915 by Lawrence Lambe, *Eoceratops* is known only from fragmentary skull material found along the Red Deer River. Its head was about one meter (three ft) long, with a short, slightly curved nasal horn and two long horns above the eyes. The horn arrangement is similar to that of *Triceratops*. Most experts think the specimen is that of a young dinosaur and have suggested that *Eoceratops* is a juvenile *Triceratops* or *Chasmosaurus*.

142

*F*ilm noir dinosaurs, a pair of Eoceratops *passes quietly beneath a red moon. It is unlikely that these animals were nocturnal, but the unusual light may have roused them. The moon would have appeared closer to the Earth during Cretaceous times than it does today.*

Arrhinoceratops
hornless nose face

Arrhinoceratops does indeed have a nose horn, but it is short and wasn't regarded as a true horn by the palaeontologist who first described it. Its frill, although slightly shorter, is similar to that of *Anchiceratops*. Rounded bones along its edge probably gave it an uneven appearance.

It is a rare fossil. Most of what we know about it comes from a nearly complete skull found near the Bleriot Ferry in the Red Deer River valley in 1923. The skull bears a puncture wound thought to be from the horn of another ceratopsian.

A cold, clear night drives sleep from Arrhinoceratops. Resting on mudflats near a flooded river, this pair displays the broad frill and the large brow horns characteristic of the genus. The similarity to Triceratops *is also evident.*

Triceratops
three-horned face

At nine meters (30 ft) in length, *Triceratops* was among the largest ceratopsians and one of the last to become extinct. It made up the bulk of the plant-eating population just before the end of the Cretaceous. Its remains are particularly common in coastal lowland sediments.

It had a single, short nasal horn and horns as long as hockey sticks protruding above its eyes. Its head, sometimes as much as three meters (10 ft) long, was the largest ever possessed by a land animal. It had large eyes and a relatively large brain. *Triceratops* was probably a feisty animal. Many specimens have bones damaged in combats with rivals or predators.

Triceratops remains were first discovered near Denver, Colorado, in 1887. At first they were identified as the remains of a recently extinct species of buffalo. The first *Triceratops* skull found in Alberta was discovered by C. M. Sternberg near Big Valley in 1946.

A classic confrontation pits Tyrannosaurus rex *against two determined* Triceratops *bulls. The solid frills and deadly horns of the ceratopsians would have created havoc for most attackers. Some fossil bones show the marks of damage and breakage, perhaps the result of combats such as this. Among the last dinosaurs of the Late Cretaceous,* Triceratops *may have preferred open woodlands to the swamps.*

The
Segnosaurs

Alberta Segnosaur Localities

The Segnosaurs
Slow Lizards

Segnosaurs, or slow lizards, are among the most recent dinosaur families to be identified. They may also prove to be among the most controversial. First unearthed in Mongolia, their remains have now been identified in Canada and the United States as well.

Segnosaurs were unusual. They could walk on their hind legs but may have spent time on all fours. They were clearly saurischian dinosaurs. Yet their hipbones were like those of ornithischians, the bird-hipped dinosaurs.

Perhaps the segnosaurs provide a link between the two major orders. They may be evolutionary throwbacks to a time when birdlike and lizardlike dinosaurs were just beginning to evolve distinguishing characteristics. Hence their name, the slow lizards.

These dinosaurs were mid-sized animals, with sturdy shoulders and a long neck. Their skulls ended in a toothless beak. Further back in the jaw was a series of short teeth.

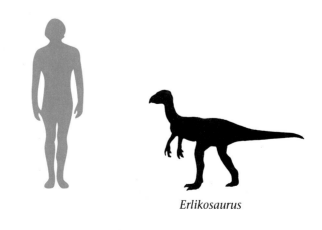

Erlikosaurus

150

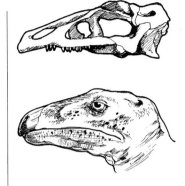

Although pointed, the teeth were also cusped, an unusual arrangement. Four sharp, narrow claws jutted out of each large hind foot. Some footprints attributed to segnosaurs suggest that their toes may have been webbed, but this is inconclusive.

We can only guess at the habits and behavior of these dinosaurs. They may have been swimmers; they may have eaten fish. On the other hand, their jaw seems to have been lightly built, and their teeth aren't the teeth of a pure carnivore. A beak possibly capped their snout. Perhaps they ate a specialized diet, as pandas and koalas do. They may have lived near rivers in the uplands. Perhaps they only migrated through Alberta. Even their size is uncertain, given the scarcity of their remains. More finds and research are necessary before we can suggest answers for the many questions that surround slow lizards.

Although Erlikosaurus *is poorly known in general, one well-preserved skull, missing only the lower jaw, has been found in Mongolia. It clearly shows the toothless beak and the spikelike teeth further back in the mouth.*

Comparison of a segnosaur pelvis with the pelvis of a typical ornithischian shows clear similarities. Nonetheless, other features have led many scientists to classify segnosaurs as saurischian, or 'lizard-hipped,' dinosaurs.

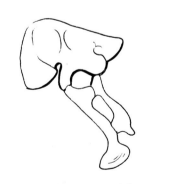

Segnosaur pelvis

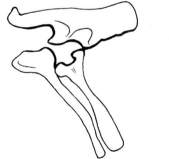

Ornithischian pelvis

140   120   100   80   65

MILLIONS OF YEARS AGO

An Alberta Segnosaur

Alberta segnosaur fossils are fragmentary. Chunks of a skull, an unusual claw and broken vertebrae, all from Dinosaur Provincial Park, are likely segnosaur remains. Additional material has been found just across the border in Montana.

Even this fragmentary material is scarce. This suggests that segnosaurs were relatively rare in Alberta. Or perhaps they lived in upland areas, only occasionally making forays onto the deltaic plain that would later become Dinosaur Provincial Park. Some of the bone fragments are waterworn, indicating that a river transported them long distances.

Erlikosaurus
Erlik's lizard

Erlikosaurus was named for Erlik, king of the dead in Mongolian mythology. A joint Soviet-Mongolian expedition first discovered *Erlikosaurus* remains in southeast Mongolia in the 1970s.

Evidence of *Erlikosaurus* in Alberta comes from a 1967 expedition to Dinosaur Provincial Park. A number of unidentified bones, clearly belonging to some then unknown dinosaur family, were collected. In 1982, Philip Currie, senior palaeontologist at the Royal Tyrrell Museum of Palaeontology, discovered an unusual claw, remarkably similar to the *Erlikosaurus* claw described from Mongolia.

*N*o one is certain what segnosaurs ate, although most agree that meat of some sort made up part of the diet. Here, Erlikosaurus *spears a fish from the water. Since so few remains of this dinosaur are known, this reconstruction is largely guesswork.*

The
Ankylosaurs

Alberta Ankylosaur Localities

The Ankylosaurs
Armored Dinosaurs

The armored dinosaurs, or ankylosaurs, had stocky legs and squat, heavy bodies. Some were about the size of a large turtle. Others were bigger than a station wagon. A mosaic of flexible armor protected their bodies and small heads. Armor even covered the eyelids of some. An array of studs, spikes and tail clubs kept their enemies at a distance.

Most ankylosaurs were built like battle tanks, with particularly wide rear ends. This was probably necessary because their legs were heavily muscled to support the animals' weight. In spite of their bulk, ankylosaurs may have been agile animals.

The expanded rear may have also contained an enlarged digestive system that helped process the wads of plant material consumed by the animal. Since ankylosaur teeth were weak, food probably underwent a minimal amount of chewing and was instead broken down by enzymes in the animal's stomach.

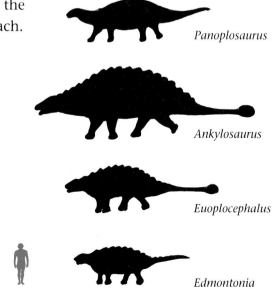

Panoplosaurus

Ankylosaurus

Euoplocephalus

Edmontonia

They were planteaters, and their unusual squared-off snouts suggest that they shuffled through the thick Late Cretaceous vegetation with their heads close to the ground, cropping low-level plants with their stubby teeth. In general, their heads were somewhat triangular and rested on the end of a short neck. Their jaws were weak, but some had particularly well-developed noses with elaborate sinuses. This may have given them a good sense of smell, or it may have enabled the dinosaur to moisten the air it was breathing, much as mammals do today.

Ankylosaurs are the only animals to have evolved tail clubs. Made of bone and manipulated by powerful tail muscles, the clubs were dangerous weapons. The club of Ankylosaurus (above) was less pronounced than that of Euoplocephalus (below), but it was larger.

Huddled together as the sand swept over them 70 million years ago, a clutch of young ankylosaurs was unearthed by a joint Canadian-Chinese team on a 1988 expedition to the Gobi Desert. Scientists from the Royal Tyrrell Museum of Palaeontology play an important role in these ongoing explorations.

157

In side view, the skull of Euoplocephalus is a sturdy helmet of bone. Slabs of bone protect the entire skull and even cover the eyelids.

The forerunner of the armored dinosaurs may have looked like *Scelidosaurus*. The back of this dinosaur was lined with seven rows of small studs. Later ankylosaurs carried this development to an extreme, developing an unusual array of spikes and plates. The only Australian ankylosaur, *Minmi*, had armor on its belly.

Two distinct ankylosaur families evolved. The ankylosaurs were robustly built, with strong limbs and broad skulls. The nodosaurs, or node lizards, were slimmer, with narrower skulls and limbs, and sharp spines on their flanks.

Among the most successful dinosaurs, ankylosaurs probably evolved in Asia and spread into North America through the Arctic. They survived for some 60 million years and were most numerous just before the great extinctions that annihilated all dinosaurs.

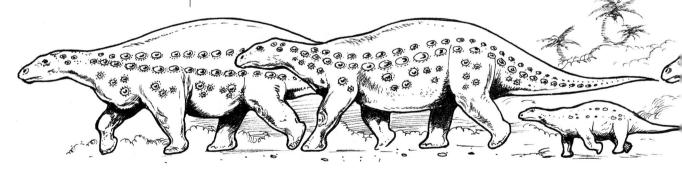

One of the earliest known ornithischian dinosaurs, Scelidosaurus retains some primitive characteristics. Its legs were pillarlike and its feet large. It may also be related to the stegosaurs.

Remains of these four-legged planteaters have been found in many parts of the world, with particularly good specimens coming from North America and Asia. Some remains have even been found in Antarctica. Most of the North American specimens are preserved upside down. Perhaps the carcasses were flipped over by large carnivores, or perhaps they gradually turned over as they bloated and their limbs stiffened. Dead cattle go through a similar process, although their body shape prevents them from turning completely over. Curiously, specimens from the Gobi Desert are less likely to be found upside down, probably because they were preserved in a different, more arid, environment.

140   120   100   80   .65

MILLIONS OF YEARS AGO

Alberta Ankylosaurs

Four different kinds of armored dinosaurs have been found in Alberta. Their remains have been found near fossils of duckbills, horned dinosaurs and carnivores such as *Albertosaurus*. The ankylosaurs from Alberta are not early models. They are rather late designs, appearing some 80 million years ago and persisting right to the Cretaceous-Tertiary Boundary. Alberta specimens are among the largest known ankylosaurs.

Ankylosaurus
fused lizard

Ankylosaurus was the last armored dinosaur to evolve. Almost as big as a battle tank, it was also among the largest, although a Mongolian specimen named *Tarchia* was probably bigger. *Ankylosaurus* was heavily armored, with bands of bony plates across its back and tail. Hard studs grew in the joints between the plates. Even its head was protected. In addition, *Ankylosaurus* possessed a formidable tail club, which probably deterred most predators. A partial *Ankylosaurus* skeleton was found by Barnum Brown near Trochu in 1911.

Many ankylosaur specimens are found lying on their back. This is perhaps not surprising, as this would have been an extremely vulnerable position for these heavily armored animals. Here, a moss-lined riverbank collapses, spilling a large Ankylosaurus into the water and almost certain death.

Euoplocephalus
true plated head

Once considered to be the same as *Ankylosaurus*, *Euoplocephalus* is now thought to be a separate animal. At six meters (20 ft) in length, it was smaller than *Ankylosaurus* but still formidable. It possessed a tail club, and rows of ridged plates lined its back. A rounded snout containing small teeth and ending in a beak clearly mark this dinosaur as a planteater. Also like *Ankylosaurus*, it had a complex nasal cavity, indicating it may have had a keen sense of smell.

Euoplocephalus was one of the most common armored dinosaurs and is one of the best known. It was first discovered in 1902 by Lawrence Lambe, who named it *Stereocephalus*. Unfortunately, *Stereocephalus* was already in use as the name of an insect, so in 1910, Lambe renamed the animal *Euoplocephalus*. All of its known remains come from Alberta.

*F*ighting off a tyrannosaur, Euoplocephalus *swings its heavyweight tail club into action. The weapon could have easily damaged the legs of the predator, even one as large as this. Leathery skin and protective armor would have made* Euoplocephalus *an unpleasant mouthful in any case.* Euoplocephalus *disappears from the fossil record about 70 million years ago.*

Panoplosaurus
fully plated lizard

Platelike armor covered it from nose to tail. Even its throat was protected by hard bones embedded in the skin. Sharp spikes ran along its sides. Its tail was clubless. Its skull differs from other ankylosaurs found in Alberta in being narrower with a pointed snout. Its nostrils were small and perhaps indicate a poorly developed sense of smell. Although a complete skeleton has not been found, the animal's size has been estimated at about seven meters (23 ft). It was abundant in Alberta some 75 million years ago.

Panoplosaurus remains were first discovered by C. M. Sternberg near Little Sandhill Creek, a tributary of the Red Deer River, in 1917. Other remains have been found in Texas and Montana.

Tempted by the blossoms of a magnolia tree, Panoplosaurus inadvertently shows off its array of armor. These dinosaurs normally grazed more closely to the ground. A stretch like this would have been dangerous for Panoplosaurus, since a fall could tip it onto its back, a position from which it could likely not recover.

Edmontonia
from Edmonton

Edmontonia was first located by George Paterson, a teamster with the 1924 Geological Survey of Canada expedition to Alberta. It was found in the Red Deer River valley some 11 kilometers (seven miles) west of the town of Morrin.

Although similar to *Panoplosaurus* in some respects, notably the panelling of protective plates fused to the skull and the squared-off muzzle, *Edmontonia* had a longer skull and different teeth. It was about two-thirds the size of *Ankylosaurus*. Like other ankylosaurs, *Edmontonia* had a short neck, a large pelvis and an arched back. Its limbs were sturdy and its feet broad.

Edmontonia *disappears into a dank forest, trailing its narrow, clubless tail. Few remains of this animal are known, perhaps because relatively few of them lived. Their weak teeth limited them to a specialized diet of pulpy foods.*

AND THEN...
THERE WERE NONE

Extinction Theories

Few animals were as widespread or as dominant as the dinosaurs. They were so abundant, so powerful, so marvellously varied. Yet they are so irretrievably dead.

What happened to them? Their bones dream within the rocks of every continent, testimony to 150 million years of vigorous life. But only in certain rocks. Any strata younger than 65 million years may contain fossil mammals, birds or fish. But no dinosaurs. They disappear, suddenly, from the fossil record at the end of the Cretaceous.

They weren't alone. Many large marine reptiles, the flying reptiles, families of shellfish and microscopic marine organisms went with them. In their wake a handful of familiar reptiles remained – crocodiles, turtles and snakes among them. Many mammals survived. So did birds and most fish.

Any theory about dinosaur extinction must account for the disappearance of so many animals and, on the other hand, explain why some survived.

Many theories have been proposed, but few are compatible with the known facts. According to all available measurements, the dinosaurs were too big for Noah's ark. Since they came in so many different shapes and sizes, it's unlikely they became too big to mate or to feed themselves. One theory holds that mammals ate the dinosaurs' eggs. But mammals and dinosaurs coexisted for millions of years. Why would the impact be felt only at the end of the Cretaceous? And why did so many marine reptiles disappear too?

It's been suggested that dinosaurs weren't fully equipped to eat the newly evolved flowering plants. But some had teeth ideally adapted to chewing up vegetable matter. Furthermore, dinosaurs ate flowering plants for 30 million years without suffering any ill effects.

Deadly epidemics may have swept the planet. But epidemics are usually selective, singling out one or two species for attack. If an epidemic wiped out the dinosaurs, why didn't it touch the turtles or the crocodiles? And why did it affect tiny invertebrate animals living in the oceans?

Perhaps the whole world changed. An unprecedented battery of volcanos may have swathed the planet in deadly ash and fumes. Or a star may have gone nova, bombarding the Earth with deadly radiation. Only those creatures able to burrow underground, or able to take refuge in deep water, survived. Or a huge asteroid, pitched through space by a primordial explosion, may have collided with the Earth. The impact lofted debris and moisture into the air, blocking out the sunlight.

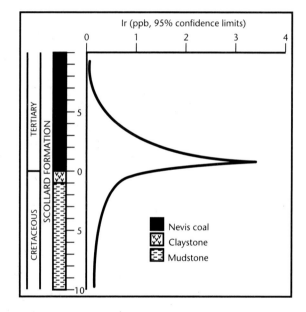

The Earth cooled, plants died and so did the planteaters. With nothing left to feed on, the large meateaters died too. When the sky cleared, the planet warmed up rapidly, causing heat stress among the few reptiles not already dead.

Other evidence points to a less dramatic finale. Plant fossils suggest the Earth was cooling off. This may have led to a gradual decrease in the dinosaur population. Although some dinosaur lines remain vigorous to the end, the group as a whole may have been in decline for half a million years.

Found at the Cretaceous-Tertiary Boundary in many parts of the world, including Alberta, is a thread of the rare element iridium. When shown on a graph, a sharp increase, or spike, is evident. Iridium is found more often on asteroids than it is on Earth and so may be evidence of a major asteroid impact.

The Eagle Butte Structure is barely visible to the human eye. In fact, most of it lies beneath the ground, under the surface of the plains near the northwest border of the Cypress Hills. Beneath the surface, the rocks are abnormal, faulted and shattered and in general disarray. Geologists have interpreted the site as the impact point of an asteroid. Evidence suggests it may have struck Earth near the end of the Cretaceous.

The sediments of Dinosaur Provincial Park do not chart a decrease in dinosaur populations. They are too old. Further upriver, however, in the younger sediments of the Trochu area, there seems to be evidence of a sparser reptilian population. Fewer dinosaurs have been found in sediments closest to the Cretaceous-Tertiary Boundary than in those 10 million years older. Among these last dinosaurs were some of the largest known in Alberta. *Triceratops*, the biggest horned dinosaur, trundled through the temperate forest. The largest land-dwelling carnivore, *Tyrannosaurus rex,* stalked across the coastal plain. But the variety wasn't what it once was, and neither was the total number.

This increasing domination of a few species may have made them more susceptible to catastrophe.

It's possible that this decline is more apparent than real. The upriver sediments haven't been prospected as thoroughly as those in Dinosaur Provincial Park. And even in the Park, a collecting bias has led to the collection of large, complete specimens while small or fragmentary remains were over-looked. So any count of specimens may be misleading. To remedy this, palaeontologists from the Royal Tyrrell Museum of Palaeontology are taking a bone census, a count of every bone. Thousands have been enumerated to date. Eventually, this will help provide a clearer picture of dinosaur demographics.

Some findings, or lack of them, suggest that dinosaurs died out first in the northern latitudes and survived longest in the equatorial zone. This too suggests that the climate was changing, with cooler winters driving the great reptiles into more restricted living quarters. A cataclysmic event, such as a supernova or an asteroid collision, may simply have been the *coup de grâce* for a population already doomed.

Some recent findings suggest that the world warmed up dramatically, in a brief reversal of the long-term cooling trend, at the end of the Cretaceous. Palaeobiologist Jack Wolfe, after studying leaf assemblages at the Cretaceous-Tertiary Boundary, has proposed that temperature rose an average of 10 degrees Celsius in a one-million-year period immediately after the Boundary. The same period experienced a sharp increase in precipitation. The combined result was a greenhouse effect. It may have been caused by an asteroid crashing into the ocean and creating huge amounts of water vapour.

We know that the Earth has had damaging asteroid impacts in the past. This crater in eastern Quebec was made about 213 million years ago at the end of the Triassic Period. Dinosaurs were alive then and survived this impact, although some other reptiles disappeared. Perhaps a more devastating impact at the Cretaceous-Tertiary Boundary was enough to wipe out the dinosaurs.

Recently, some researchers have argued that dinosaurs did not all die at the end of the Cretaceous. Some may have survived into the next era. Finds in Montana and New Mexico as well as other parts of the world confirm dinosaur remains in Paleocene deposits. Most scientists, however, continue to think that these fossils washed into the Palaeocene sediments from older rocks.

At this point, we cannot identify a single cause for dinosaur extinction. We may never be able to. And in the long run, the secret to dinosaur success may be far more important than the reasons for their demise.

Finding Dinosaurs

Dinosaur bones are fossils. The term originally referred to any unusual object dug out of the ground. Today, however, only the traces of living organisms or their activities are known as fossils.

People have been finding fossils for centuries. A record of 'dragon bones' shows up in China as early as the third century A.D. Ancient Egyptians used fossil wood in making corduroy roads. In North America, Navaho Indians considered petrified logs to be the bones of giants, whose blood lay congealed in nearby lava flows. Blackfoot tribes in Alberta, seeing the huge bones in the badlands, thought of them as the remains of ancestral buffalo. Some Indians carried fossil bones in their medicine bundles.

In England, an Oxford professor described a massive dinosaur leg bone in 1667. At first he thought it belonged to an elephant brought to England by the Romans, but eventually he was persuaded that it came from a human giant.

Noah's raven or a dinosaur? Dinosaur tracks were known as early as 1800 in Connecticut. Locals considered them to be the footprints of a large bird, perhaps a raven that Noah had on his ark.

By the early 1800s many bones and teeth were being unearthed, but there really weren't any dinosaurs. The word dinosaur wasn't coined until 1841, when Richard Owen, putting together the Greek words for 'terrible' and 'lizard,' suggested the name. It stuck. Because by this time, the remains of these ancient creatures had captured attention on both sides of the Atlantic.

The first North American dinosaurs were described in 1856, after teeth found in Montana were sent to the University of

Pennsylvania for study. In 1858, an almost complete hadrosaur skeleton was found in a quarry in New Jersey. This spurred men like Edward Drinker Cope and Othniel Charles Marsh, who soon began a rivalry that would make them the most famous dinosaur hunters of their time. They explored the American West in the late 1800s, unearthing tons of dinosaur bones, naming 130 new species and setting off one of the most virulent disputes in the annals of palaeontology.

Dinosaurs in Alberta

The first documented discovery of dinosaurs in Alberta came in 1874. An expedition headed by George Mercer Dawson, surveying the Canada-United States boundary, found fragments in the sandstone bluffs along the Milk River. Ten years later, Joseph Burr Tyrrell discovered the first dinosaur skull in the Red Deer River valley. It was the first known specimen of an *Albertosaurus*.

Word of Tyrrell's discovery got around. Fossil hunters began probing the Red Deer River valley with increasing frequency. The badlands that spread from its banks are a fascinating, eerie terrain. French settlers called the arid slopes *mauvaises terres* because they were difficult to cross and impossible to farm. Further south, Sioux Indians had called it *Mako Sika,* or 'land bad,' for centuries. The pillared, fluted landscape, scorched by the relentless prairie sun, was tough going for the bone hunters. They soon learned that the best way to explore the badlands was by boat.

Wealthy and intractable, Othniel Charles Marsh (1831–1899) hired crews of fossil hunters to explore the still untamed American West and ship specimens back to Yale University. Among the specimens he introduced to the world were Ornithomimus *and* Triceratops. *In 1870, Marsh pointed out that Cope had reconstructed a long-necked plesiosaur with the head on the tail of the animal. Cope never forgave him.*

The flatboat Barnum Brown constructed in Red Deer in 1910 was 10 meters (32 ft) long. At each end was a seven meter (22 ft) sweep, used to steer the craft around rapids and sand bars. Heavy rain and a lack of suitable camping sites forced the expedition to use the boat as a houseboat.

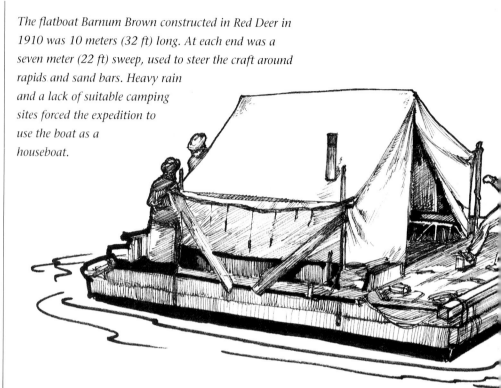

Thomas Chesmer Weston, who had seen the valley earlier, was the first bone hunter to use the river as a means of travel. Excited by news of Tyrrell's finds, Weston returned to the river in 1888. On the advice of Reverend Leonard Gaetz of Red Deer, he used that city as a staging area for his expedition.

He had a boat built, but it sank 13 kilometers (eight miles) downstream. A local farmer, Roderick McKenzie, hauled the crew out of the water and promised to build them a better boat the following year. Weston returned and made a successful run of the river in 1889. He identified the badlands of what is now Dinosaur Provincial Park as a great potential source of dinosaur remains, although he took few specimens back to Ottawa with him.

In the spring of 1909, an Alberta rancher visiting in New York tipped off Barnum Brown to the wealth of dinosaur remains in the Red Deer River valley. The following summer,

Brown headed north. He worked the Red Deer River until 1915, sending most of his finds to the American Museum of Natural History in New York.

There were a few complaints. Why should Canadian dinosaurs leave the country to enrich displays few Canadians could ever see and to stimulate research few Canadians could ever take part in? Responding to these complaints, the Geological Survey of Canada soon placed its own party in the field. It too was led by an American, Charles Hazelius Sternberg. But the specimens stayed in Canada.

Sternberg worked the valley with a field wagon and a variety of boats. His first expedition made use of a rowboat built in Calgary. The following year he had a scow built in Drumheller. He pitched two tents on it and bought another boat with a five horsepower motor to tow it.

Sternberg, often working with his sons, operated in the Red Deer River valley until 1917. Each year brought additional finds, some of which were species never seen before. His party

Brilliant, short-tempered and plagued by nightmares, Edward Drinker Cope (1840–1897) had been interested in fossils from age six. His workers found such dinosaurs as Allosaurus *and* Monoclonius *in relatively unexplored parts of Colorado and Montana. Many of Cope's dinosaurs can be seen at the American Museum of Natural History in New York.*

Some say Jean L'Heureux was chased out of Quebec for corrupting the morals of society. Other rumors claim he attempted to pose as a doctor in Winnipeg and, when found out, had to flee across the American border. He eventually settled with the Blackfoot Indians and became their official interpreter. On his travels, he noted the bones of large animals in the Red Deer River badlands years before Tyrrell's discoveries. He recorded the native belief about the bones:

"The natives say that the grandfather of the buffalo is buried here. They honor these remains by offering presents as a means of making the spirit which gave them life to help them in their hunt."

was the first to discover dinosaurs such as *Styracosaurus* and *Chasmosaurus*. Many of Sternberg's discoveries can now be seen in the Canadian Museum of Nature in Ottawa.

When Sternberg and Brown left the Red Deer River, the first golden age of dinosaur collecting in Alberta was over. World wars, the Depression and indifference intervened. But in recent years, collecting in Alberta has accelerated once again.

Much of this collecting has focused on Dinosaur Provincial Park, some 48 kilometers (30 miles) northeast of Brooks. There, constantly eroding sediments disclose an unequalled lode of fossils. Teeth, shells, leaves, the trunks of ancient trees, fish scales and dinosaur bones come out of the Earth. Complete skeletons are still being discovered. The Park is such a trove of ancient remains that it has been declared a World Heritage Site by the United Nations.

Recently, collecting has proven successful in other parts of the province as well. Devil's Coulee, south of Lethbridge, was identified as an important site in 1987, after a young girl found fragments of dinosaur eggs in the area. Concentrated collecting has unearthed dinosaur eggs, baby bones and a variety of other fossils.

"I know of no wilder or more fascinating scenery," *said Charles Hazelius Sternberg (1850–1943) when he entered the Alberta badlands in 1912. A staunch Lutheran and 62 years of age when he came to Canada, Sternberg was already a well-known fossil collector. When he died, he had collected more dinosaurs than any other person.*

Further north, along the Pipestone Creek near Grande Prairie, a massive bonebed was opened by the Tyrrell Museum in 1986. Known as early as 1974 by local collectors, no one had previously excavated it. The bonebed has given up hundreds of bones from *Pachyrhinosaurus*, a large horned dinosaur. Young dinosaurs are found in abundance here, and the find has answered some long-standing questions about the shape of this dinosaur's frill. It has disclosed information about growth and variation in these dinosaurs and, like most digs, the Pipestone Creek site offers some important fringe benefits – plant fossils and amber have also been discovered there.

In 1988, dinosaur bones were spied protruding from the river bank near Edmonton. Even more recent finds in the foothills and in the southeast corner of the province promise an array of new bones and possibly new ideas about the dinosaurs' world.

Some people have spent their life looking for dinosaurs. Many palaeontologists endure extreme cold, taxing bureaucracy, awful travel arrangements, hemorrhoids and mosquitos just to find one more bone, one more tooth, one more egg. Perhaps it will make them famous; most likely it won't. They can rarely describe why they do it.

In Alberta the obsession has been rewarded time and time again. As this book has shown, the dinosaurs from Alberta are one of the most amazing prehistoric faunas. As erosion gnaws the badlands away, exposing new and different bones on the surface, more and more of them are collected and examined, and so they enter the parade of great vanished reptiles that continues to expand our knowledge of the past and enrich our present lives.

Ambitious but partially deaf, the young Joseph Burr Tyrrell (1858–1957) showed little promise of his later career. One of his first assignments with the Geological Survey of Canada in western Canada was to make a pace survey. He had to walk all day, usually alone, and keep an accurate count of his steps. After his discovery of coal and dinosaur bones in the Red Deer River valley, he went on to become a important Arctic explorer.

Alberta Dinosaurs: Where to See Them

Dinosaurs from Alberta are fixtures in some of the world's best-loved museums. The list below is not exhaustive, but it does indicate most of the better known displays of Alberta dinosaurs.

Dinosaur	Where to See It
Albertosaurus	Royal Tyrrell Museum of Palaeontology, Drumheller, Alberta
	Royal Ontario Museum, Toronto, Ontario
	Canadian Museum of Nature, Ottawa, Ontaio
	Field Museum of Natural History, Chicago, Illinois
	Smithsonian, Washington, D.C.
Anatosaurus	University of Wyoming Geology Museum, Wyoming
	Senckenburg Natural History Museum, Frankfurt, West Germany
	Denver Museum of Natural History, Denver, Colorado
	University of Michigan Museum of Palaeontology, Michigan
	American Museum of Natural History, New York, N.Y.
Anchiceratops	Canadian Museum of Nature, Ottawa, Ontario
	Field Museum of Natural History, Chicago, Illinois
	American Museum of Natural History, New York, N.Y.
	University of Wyoming Geology Museum, Wyoming
Ankylosaurus	Provincial Museum of Alberta, Edmonton, Alberta
	American Museum of Natural History, New York, N.Y.
Arrhinoceratops	Royal Ontario Museum, Toronto, Ontario
Brachylophosaurus	National Museum of Nature, Ottawa, Ontario
Caenagnathus	Royal Tyrrell Museum of Palaeontology, Drumheller, Alberta
Centrosaurus	Royal Tyrrell Museum of Palaeontology, Drumheller, Alberta
	American Museum of Natural History, New York, N.Y.
	Museum of La Plata University, La Plata, Argentina

Dinosaur	Where to See It
Chasmosaurus	Royal Tyrrell Museum of Palaeontology, Drumheller, Alberta
	Royal Ontario Museum, Toronto, Ontario
	Canadian Museum of Nature, Ottawa, Ontario
	American Museum of Natural History, New York, N.Y.
Corythosaurus	Royal Tyrrell Museum of Palaeontology, Drumheller, Alberta
	Provincial Museum of Alberta, Edmonton, Alberta
	Royal Ontario Museum, Toronto, Ontario
	American Museum of Natural History, New York, N.Y.
	Academy of Natural Sciences, Philadelphia, Pennsylvania
Daspletosaurus	Canadian Museum of Nature, Ottawa, Ontario
Dromaeosaurus	Royal Tyrrell Museum of Palaeontology, Drumheller, Alberta
Dromiceiomimus	Canadian Museum of Nature, Ottawa, Ontario
Edmontonia	Royal Tyrrell Museum of Palaeontology, Drumheller, Alberta
Edmontosaurus	Drumheller & District Fossil Museum, Drumheller, Alberta
	Royal Tyrrell Museum of Palaeontology, Drumheller, Alberta
	Royal Ontario Museum, Toronto, Ontario
	Senckenburg Natural History Museum, Frankfurt, West Germany
	Los Angeles County Museum, Los Angeles, California
Eoceratops	University of Alberta, Edmonton, Alberta
Euoplocephalus	British Museum of Natural History, London, U.K.
Gryposaurus	Royal Tyrrell Museum of Palaeontology, Drumheller, Alberta
	Canadian Museum of Nature, Ottawa, Ontario

Dinosaur	Where to See It	Dinosaur	Where to See It
Hypacrosaurus	Royal Tyrrell Museum of Palaeontology, Drumheller, Alberta Canadian Museum of Nature, Ottawa, Ontario	Parksosaurus	Royal Ontario Museum, Toronto, Ontario
Kritosaurus	Royal Tyrrell Museum of Palaeontology, Drumheller, Alberta Royal Ontario Museum, Toronto, Ontario Pratt Museum, Amherst, Massachusetts	Prosaurolophus	Royal Ontario Museum, Toronto, Ontario Smithsonian, Washington, D.C.
		Saurolophus	American Museum of Natural History, New York, N.Y.
Lambeosaurus	Royal Tyrrell Museum of Palaeontology, Drumheller, Alberta Provincial Museum of Alberta, Edmonton, Alberta Royal Ontario Museum, Toronto, Ontario American Museum of Natural History, New York, N.Y. Field Museum of Natural History, Chicago, Illinois	Stegoceras	Royal Tyrrell Museum of Palaeontology, Drumheller, Alberta University of Alberta, Edmonton, Alberta
		Struthiomimus	Provincial Museum of Alberta, Edmonton, Alberta Royal Ontario Museum, Toronto, Ontario American Museum of Natural History, New York, N.Y.
Leptoceratops	Canadian Museum of Nature, Ottawa, Ontario	Styracosaurus	Canadian Museum of Nature, Ottawa, Ontario American Museum of Natural History, New York, N.Y.
Maiasaura	Museum of the Rockies, Bozeman, Montana	Thescelosaurus	Canadian Museum of Nature, Ottawa, Ontario
Montanoceratops	Royal Tyrrell Museum of Palaeontology, Drumheller, Alberta American Museum of Natural History, New York, N.Y.	Triceratops	Royal Tyrrell Museum of Palaeontology, Drumheller, Alberta Canadian Museum of Nature, Ottawa, Ontario American Museum of Natural History, New York, N.Y. Smithsonian, Washington, D.C. Museum of the Rockies, Bozeman, Montana
Ornithomimus	Royal Ontario Museum, Toronto, Ontario American Museum of Natural History, New York, N.Y.		
Pachycephalosaurus	American Museum of Natural History, New York, N.Y.	Troodon	Canadian Museum of Nature, Ottawa, Ontario
Pachyrhinosaurus	Drumheller and District Fossil Museum, Drumheller, Alberta	Tyrannosaurus rex	Royal Tyrrell Museum of Palaeontology, Drumheller, Alberta American Museum of Natural History, New York, N.Y. Carnegie Museum of Natural History, Pittsburgh, Pennsylvania Los Angeles County Museum, Los Angeles, California
Panoplosaurus	Canadian Museum of Nature, Ottawa, Ontario American Museum of Natural History, New York, N.Y.		
Parasaurolophus	Royal Tyrrell Museum of Palaeontology, Drumheller, Alberta Royal Ontario Museum, Toronto, Ontario		

General Index

NAME INDEX

183